# Brian Howe

# Portfolio

## Case Studies for Business English

## Teacher's Guide

**Longman Group UK Limited,**
*Longman House, Burnt Mill, Harlow,*
*Essex CM20 2JE, England*
*and Associated Companies throughout the world*

First published 1988
ISBN 0 582 85247 1

Set in 9 on 11 pt Adobe Helvetica

Page preparation by Comind, Cambridge
Printed in Great Britain
by Mackays of Chatham

# Contents

# Introduction

## Aims

*Portfolio* is a series of business case studies designed to activate communication between students of Business English. Each of the 15 main cases presents an open-ended business problem which students must discuss and analyze before moving on to formulate a solution. The six *Pause for thought* sections present springboards for shorter discussions or activities.

The main aim of this book is to engage students in the communicative activities central to managerial problem-solving situations. It is assumed that students will have acquired much of the language needed to perform these activities in earlier parts of their courses. *Portfolio* allows the students to practise and refine this language in challenging and realistic management contexts.

## Teaching approach

### The case study approach

A case study approach is adopted for all or part of the units. Students proceed as outsiders through the materials and then hold a round table discussion to summarize the problems and arrive at appropriate solutions. A typical approach would be:

1 **Pre-teach relevant language.** Key language exponents, e.g. *The language of information presentation*, are presented in the *Language reference unit* of the *Student's Book*.
2 **Set the scene.** Identify the students' target activities e.g. to hold a meeting to solve a problem of budgeting for Oxfam. Then open the case with the necessary case background as set out in the opening paragraphs of the units.
3 **Study the facts.** Students should ask and answer the questions which precede each exhibit. This may lead to individual reports on the exhibit and short discussions in which students interpret the documents and build up the case step by step.
4 **Describe the emerging situation.** As students proceed, they should begin to form opinions about the emerging situation and link the exhibits into a whole.
5 **Identify the problem.** Once the exhibits have been analyzed, students should identify the key problems. The discussion should therefore move away from individual exhibits towards the overall situation.

6 **Identify possible solutions.** Students should present a range of possible solutions and compare these in terms of their advantages and disadvantages.
7 **Select and justify the best solution.** Students should now argue their points of view, attempt to persuade each other to accept their ideas and make the appropriate compromises to reach a solution.

### The simulation approach

This approach to these cases involves the students taking the roles of participants in the case studies. The *Student's Book* instructions indicate where this happens in a unit, and this book gives more ideas on where this approach can be taken.

### Teacher's Guide contents

The *Teacher's Guide* units have the following structure.

1 **Synopsis** This summarizes the content of the unit.
2 **Case objectives** This lists the main business targets of the unit.
3 **Language objectives** This lists the overall language targets of the unit.
4 **Suggested preparation** In this section ideas about how to prepare the students, open the case and exploit its main features are suggested.
5 **Classroom management** Case study or simulation and role play approaches to the unit are suggested.
6 **Page summaries** These indicate the target activities for the students on each page of the case.
7 **Exhibit titles** For ease of reference, these relate directly to the exhibit on the *Student's Book* page. Each title contains the following:
a) **Language objectives** - a list of the main language items to be exploited with that particular exhibit.
b) **Target lexis** - a list of the key lexical items relating to that exhibit.
c) **Answers to questions** - relating to the focus questions which precede each exhibit on the *Student's Book* page.
d) **Further questions** - these are designed to stimulate further discussion of the exhibit and to deepen the student's knowledge of the situation.
e) **Target student commentary** - these are designed to present the ideal description of a particular exhibit. As such, they may be used as a reference point for the student's own summary or simply as a quick resumé of the exhibit. By reading the commentaries in quick succession, you will be able to assimilate the main features of the case very quickly.
f) **Likely outcome** - this section suggests the possible outcome of the case.

## Synopsis

A Canadian shorthaul airline, catering mainly for the business traveller, tries to increase its revenue on its most important route by filling more seats. It does this by offering special reduced fares. The new fare structure causes its existing business customers to transfer to the railways. The airline has to devise a plan to win back those customers and yet fill the empty seats.

## Case objectives

1 Identifying the two main problems facing airlines:
  a) filling sets; b) maximizing revenue.
2 Identifying the way that seat filling strategies can damage revenue maximizing strategies, i.e. to fill seats prices must be reduced. Lower prices could mean less revenue.
3 Finding ways of reconciling these two objectives.

## Overall language objectives

1 Comparing the features and benefits of service products.
2 Interpreting diagrammatic information.
3 Presenting the thinking behind an advertising campaign.
4 Analyzing, discussing, presenting and resolving the central issues behind a service industry marketing problem.

## Suggested preparation

Ask students to prepare a short presentation of items of *realia* from this unit for homework prior to the classroom exploitation of the case. For example, different students could be asked to study the InterAir advertisement on page 1, the railway advertisement and the airport conversation on the cassette on page 2. The students could then present the information from these items to the class prior to the start of the case study. In this way students would have a grasp of the starting situation and could, if class time is limited, move rapidly onto the central problem as depicted in the diagrams on page 3.

As this case is relevant to any business person who flies regularly, a suitable warm-up approach may be to question students about their own flying experiences and preferences, e.g. *Did anyone fly here? How often do you fly? Do you have a favourite airline? What class do you usually travel? What problems have you had flying? Do you like flying?*

## Classroom management

Pages 1 and 2 follow the case study approach. Students present their interpretations of the three diagrams on page 3 to the rest of the class and on page 4 take part in an InterAir Planning Group meeting.

---

## Page 1 **Bottoms on seats**

---

Students read the background to the situation, study an airline advertisement and listen to the airline's recorded information service.

From the opening narrative, elicit the central problem faced by InterAir, i.e. spare capacity on its most lucrative route. Then lead into the airline's advertisement.

## The fastest way to business and pleasure in Toronto

### Language objectives

1 Identifying and describing the main selling points of a product or service, e.g. *The main selling point is ease of booking and speed of travel.*
2 Identifying the target readers of an advertisement, e.g. *This advertisement is aimed at two kinds of people, primarily the business traveller but also the non-business traveller.*
3 Interpreting and explaining the strategy behind an advertisement, e.g. *What they're trying to do is fill their spare capacity.*

### Target Lexis

| | | |
|---|---|---|
| advertisement | advantage | benefit |
| conditions | discount fare | feature |
| frills | target reader | |

### Answers to questions

2 The main selling points on this route are the instant booking facilities and the speed of travel.
3 The main 'frills' are free drinks, breakfast and newspapers.
4 The special offer is the new, low fare for travellers who can book ahead.

## Further questions

1 What kind of person is InterAir's main customer?
*The business person.*
2 What are their specific needs on this route?
*Speed, frequency of services, reliability, instant booking.*
3 Why does InterAir have spare capacity on this route?
*Because there are not enough business travellers to fill each flight.*
4 How is InterAir going to attract non-business passengers?
*By offering special bargain fares.*

## Target student commentary

InterAir's main selling points on this route are obviously speed and frequency of flights. Its main customers, business people, clearly want a quick, reliable and highly flexible service and they are willing to pay a high price for this. In addition to these features, InterAir also offers various 'frills' such as breakfast, free drinks and newspapers. InterAir is also offering a variety of special discount fares with the aim of filling excess capacity on these business flights. But these discount fares have special booking conditions attached to them.

## InterAir's recorded information service

### Language objectives

1 Listening to and summarizing recorded information.
2 Explaining a price structure, e.g. *The top price gives you instant booking and a guaranteed seat.*

See page 79 of the *Student's Book* for the tapescript.

### Answers to questions

2 The Business Class ticket costs $130 round trip while the Economy Class Fare is $70 round trip. The Advance Economy Class ticket costs $55 round trip and the Standby ticket is $20 one way.
3 Business Class has no reservation restrictions and a seat is guaranteed at all times. For the Economy Class ticket a reservation must be made three weeks in advance. The reservation condition for Advance Economy Class is three months. No reservations are possible for Standby and tickets are subject to availability.

### Further question

How do the restrictions on the non-business tickets allow the airline to reduce the prices for those tickets?
*The airline can plan ahead, restrict discount travellers to off-peak periods and maximize the number of Business Class seats available at well-known business peak periods.*

# Page 2
# A customer complains and the competition responds

Students listen to a conversation between two businessmen at Toronto airport and study a TransCanadian Rail advertisement.

## The conversation overheard at Toronto Airport

### Target lexis

| | | |
|---|---|---|
| to be dissatisfied | treatment | service |
| to complain | higher standards | expect |
| to treat | | |

See page 79 of the *Student's Book* for the tapescript

### Answers to questions

2 The main problems are the long queues, overcrowding, and the small, uncomfortable seats in the aircraft. Also, he objects to the fact that he is not separated from the non-business passengers.
3 He suggests that he complains to the airline.

### Target student commentary

The businessman is clearly very dissatisfied with the service on the Montreal-Toronto route. Although he is paying a premium price for this journey, the only advantage he can see is the instant booking. For this money he expects a much higher standard of service. In particular, he would expect to have a cabin separated off from the discount passengers, larger and more comfortable seats, and to receive generally better treatment. He intends to make a complaint to the airline.

## Six ways to improve an airline

### Language objectives

1 Describing the major feature of a service, e.g. *The major features here are comfort and personalized service.*
2 Describe the benefits of those features, e.g. *The main benefits are that the business person can travel and work in a relaxing environment.*
3 Comparing those benefits and features with competitive services, e.g. *Although the railway is slower, it is more comfortable and allows the business person to use the travel time more efficiently.*
4 Analyzing and discussing the strategy behind an advertisement, e.g. *The main strategy here is to exploit the airline's major weaknesses.*

## Target lexis

competitor    to exploit a weak point    to persuade
competitive    to play on    to outweigh
advantage    strength    to cancel out

## Answers to questions

2 The main advantages of rail travel are the relaxing views of the countryside, personalized hostess service, desks to work at, comfort and lower prices.
3 The main reason for InterAir's problems is that the railway offers genuine first class service which allows the business person to work while travelling.

## Further questions

1 What is the main disadvantage of the rail journey?
*It takes longer than the flight.*
2 What is the time differential between the air and rail services?
*About 45 minutes if you assume the plane leaves at 8 a.m.*

## Target student commentary

TransCanadian Rail is clearly trying to win business passengers from InterAir. It has found the weak points in InterAir's service and is emphasizing the comfort, personalized service and lower prices of its own service. The implication is that InterAir's planes are now overcrowded and that the business person is treated no differently from any other passenger. On the railway, by contrast, the business person can relax, do their work and arrive at their destination only a little later than if they flew by air. The message is that the benefits of rail outweigh the disadvantage of longer travelling time.

---

# Page 3
# InterAir changes course
# A new image, a new slogan

---

Students reach the core of the problem. They read the narrative link, study the changing travel patterns between Toronto and Montreal, compare journey times and analyze the impact that InterAir's new price structure has had on its own revenue.

At this point you allocate the three diagrams for study by different groups. When this has been done, the groups can come together to pool the results of their studies.

# Montreal-Toronto route analysis

## Language objectives

1 Describing pie charts, e.g. *60% of business travellers go by road.*
2 Making year-on-year comparisons, e.g. *This year the number of business travellers preferring air transport fell by 5%.*
3 Summarizing statistical trends, e.g. *There has been a marked shift away from road and air towards rail travel.*

## Target lexis

pie chart    figures    market share
segment    pattern    in absolute terms
proportion    to switch    loss of revenue
brackets

## Answers to questions

1 Business travellers are changing from air and road travel to rail travel. Every day 175 people who travelled by air last year now travel by rail. The same number has also transferred from road transport to rail.
2 The major winner is the railway. They have gained an extra 350 passengers per day.

## Further questions

1 How many business travellers use the airline per day?
*350.*
2 How many business travellers use the railway per day?
*1,050.*
3 What is the total market for daily business journeys on this route?
*3,500.*

## Target student commentary

Last year 15% of all business travellers used the airlines for this journey. This year this has fallen to 10%. There has clearly been a switch away from the airline towards the railway. In absolute terms the airline has lost 175 passengers per day or 54,600 per year. The total loss of Business Class revenue to the airline was therefore about $7m.

# Comparative breakdown of journey times

## Language objectives

1 Describing a bar chart, e.g. *The top bar represents/ gives you/shows business journeys by air.*
2 Interpreting bar charts, e.g. *The major component of the air journey is the non-flight element.*

## Target lexis

breakdown      to have the advantage over
to break down      to take (time)
component      to have the edge on

## Answers to questions

1 The airline's main strengths are the short flight time and the short total journey time. Its main weaknesses are the journey times to the airport and city centre and the check-in time. The railway's main strength is its quick access to the city centre. Its main weakness is the long total journey time. The road's main strength is that it's flexible. Its main weaknesses are the long total journey time and access to the city centre.

## Further questions

1 What proportion of the air journey is flying time? *About 30%.*
2 Why is the non-flying component so large? *Long check-in and airport access times.*

## Target student commentary

Although air travel is much faster than road or rail, this advantage is reduced by the long periods of time needed to travel to the airport, check in and travel from the destination airport to city centre. In the end, rail travel is only about 25% slower than air travel. One of the main ways to maximize their speed advantage is to reduce the non-flying time component, for example by eliminating check-in and by providing a fast coach service to the airport.

## InterAir price structure

### Language objectives

1 Comparing and contrasting categories on a year-on-year basis, e.g. *The proportion of Business Class tickets has fallen from 30% to 20% over the year.*
2 Expressing results in numerical terms, e.g. *The changing pattern of ticket sales resulted in a fall in revenue of $948 per flight.*
3 Expressing cause and effect, e.g. *The increased load factors led to a fall in revenue.*
4 Interpreting information, e.g. *This clearly suggests that the seat price discounting strategies have raised load factors but reduced revenue.*

### Target lexis

discount fares     spare capacity     revenue
price structure     load factor     loss
peak period     yield     to compensate for
off-peak     to fluctuate     to differentiate
standby     to drop

## Answers to questions

1 Last year they offered only two classes of ticket—Business Class $130 and Standard Economy Class $80. This year the airline divided the latter class into three separate classes—Economy, Advance Economy and Standby. This change has resulted in a reduction in the number of business travellers from 30% to 20%, an increase in the number of discount passengers from 50% to 79% and a reduction of spare capacity from 20% to 1%.
2 The main beneficiaries of this have been the discount passengers, especially those at the lower end of this market, standby passengers.
3 Last year average revenue per flight = $9,480. This year average revenue per flight = $8,532.

## Further questions

1 What is the average revenue loss per flight this year compared to last year? *$948.*
2 What is the total revenue loss per 52 week year? *52 x 7 x 9 x $948 $3,105,648.*
3 Why can't the airline create a permanent fixed Business Class Cabin for its prime customers? *Because the booking patterns fluctuate dramatically between daily peak and off-peak periods.*

## Target student commentary

Clearly there has been a shift towards the low price, discount fares with top price business fares accounting now for 20% of seats as against 30% for last year. This has resulted in a loss of Business Class revenue of about $7m. However, the increase in discount passengers has compensated for this to some extent and so the overall drop in revenues amounts to about $3.1m for this year. Thus, although load factors have gone up from 80% to 99%, the airline's revenues or yields have fallen. The crux of the problem is how to separate and differentiate business travellers from discount travellers in order to justify the higher price when the ticket demand patterns fluctuate so widely during any one day.

---

# Page 4 Getting to the bottom of things

Students read some of the suggestions put forward by the airline's management to solve the problem and then take part in an InterAir Planning Group meeting at which they must decide the best way to deal with the situation.

Alternatively, you may want to complete the unit as a case study and not ask the students to take part in a simulation.

# Five suggestions

## Language objectives

1 Expressing points of view, e.g. *My opinion is that...*
2 Agreeing and disagreeing with points of view, e.g. *I agree/disagree with your view that...*
3 Supporting viewpoints with evidence/arguments, e.g. *I think she's right because the basic problem is to predict demand accurately.*
4 Making recommendations/suggestions, e.g. *I'd recommend that they convert the whole aircraft to the wide seats.*

There are no comprehension questions on the five suggestions on the *Student's Book* page as they are intended as background to the meeting which closes the unit. But the following approach is suggested. Ask students to read and discuss the various management suggestions. Elicit or suggest some of the points given below:

### Suggestion 1  Separation by curtain
*For:* Offers separation/flexibility. Business cabin could be expanded and contracted as required on any one flight.
*Against:* Seats still narrow. Would not be flexible if total fixed bookings for discount passengers made it impossible to accommodate demand for business seats on any particular flight.

### Suggestion 2  Convert a proportion of seats
*For:* Would provide a certain number of comfortable Business Class seats.
*Against:* Fixed cabin would be empty on some flights and reduce number of discount fares that could be offered. On other flights it would restrict number of Business Class seats that could be sold.

### Suggestion 3  Convert whole aircraft to wide seats
*For:* Seat comfort and service standards would satisfy all passengers.
*Against:* More costly. Each wide seat reduces total aircraft seat capacity.

### Suggestion 4  Demand Forecasting
*For:* If used in conjunction with the flexible curtain, could predict demand for each flight on basis of exact flight in previous periods. If forecasts accurate, could result in efficient allocation of tickets and discount reservations, i.e. very few allowed on high peak flights.
*Against:* All depends on very precise forecasting.

### Suggestion 5  Ground facility improvements
*For:* Speeds up non-flight components of journey for business people. Separates from discount travellers. Pampers the business traveller.
*Against:* On its own still does not overcome in-flight problems of separation, overcrowding and seat width.

# InterAir planning group meeting agenda

Students hold a meeting as InterAir managers in some of or all of the following roles:
1 President (strategy)
2 Sales and Advertising
3 Market Research
4 Technical Support (computers, ground facilities, in-flight facilities)
5 Finance/Accounts (revenues, pricing and profitability)

## Language objectives

See *3 Meetings* in the *Language reference unit* on page ix.

## Likely Outcome

The core business problem in this case is the question of product differentiation. InterAir is selling four different products on this route at four different prices. Potential buyers of the top price product, business people, do not see sufficient product differences between Business Class and the other classes to justify the premium charge. InterAir's target therefore should be to make the product features more apparent and worthwhile. At the moment, the airline is trying to be all things to all people. Basically, it has to decide whether it is a business airline or a general airline. The premium prices that can be sustained if it can prove its suitability to the business person would seem to show that a business airline would be more profitable on this route than a general airline. To achieve this status, though, the airline must widen its seats, improve ground and in-flight services and go all out to not only win back its lost business clientele but to take a further market share from the railway and roads.

# Unit 2  Safety first

## Synopsis

The Personnel Director of a large construction company is requested by his Chairman to investigate his company's poor accident record. The Personnel Director collates the statistics, analyzes the causes and interviews staff. On the basis of these findings, the company must decide how to improve its safety standards.

## Case objectives

1 Discussing cause and effect with regard to accidents in industry.
2 Discussing the organization of a typical industrial working day and the effects this may have upon safety and output.
3 Talking about the psychological aspects of safety in the workplace, e.g. motivation, morale, incentives, with a view to devising an industrial safety campaign.

## Overall language objectives

1 Presenting information from graphs.
2 Analyzing and expressing cause and effect on the basis of statistical information.
3 Expressing inference, e.g. *This suggests that...*
4 Describing the psychology of work, e.g. *boredom, motivation, demotivation, incentive.*
5 Talking about prevention, e.g. *warning, reminding, encouraging, publicizing, motivating.*

## Suggested preparation

Make sure students are familiar with the language of *Information presentation.* (See page vii in the *Language Reference Unit.*)
   As a warm-up activity, ask students about dangers in industry, e.g. *Which are the most dangerous occupations?* Ask why accidents happen. Elicit the key lexis, e.g. *carelessness, faults, negligence.*

## Classroom management

All three pages of this unit follow a case study approach. As a final activity, students could be asked to take roles in the company at the safety meeting which concludes the unit on page 7. The roles could be a) Anderson the Chairman – he wants to improve safety without spending money or reducing working time; b) Evans, the Personnel Director – he wants to demonstrate his understanding of the facts; c) a representative of the Work's Committee – he wants to get as many concessions as possible from management.

## Page 5  Safety First

Students read the background to the situation and study a graph. From the opening narrative and speech bubbles, elicit the main problem, i.e. an unacceptably high number of accidents.

## Reported accidents graph

### Language objectives

1 Describing a statistical pattern, e.g. *The morning accident peak is just before the tea break.*
2 Interpreting a statistical pattern, e.g. *The accident peaks may be due to lack of concentration just before tea breaks.*

### Target lexis

| | | |
|---|---|---|
| axis | to occur | to concentrate |
| horizontal | to rise | fatigue |
| vertical | to fall | tiredness |
| to clock on/off | overtime | |

### Answers to questions

2 The main accident peaks are just after the morning and afternoon clocking-on times, just before the morning and afternoon tea breaks and just before the end of the normal working day.
3 The main accident troughs are after tea breaks and during the overtime period.
4 See *Target student commentary* below.

### Further questions

1 How long is each of the six uninterrupted working periods during the day?
   *1st = 2.5 hrs. 2nd = 1.25 hrs. 3rd = 1.75 hrs. 4th = 2 hrs. 5th = 1.25 hrs. 6th = 1.5 hrs.*
2 How might the length of the work period affect safety?
   *People possibly get tired or lose concentration after 1.25 hours of work.*
3 What effect do the work breaks have on safety?
   *If the preceding work period is longer than 1.25 hours, it possibly causes pre-break accident peaks, perhaps because the worker relaxes in anticipation of the break.*
4 What factors might cause the post clocking-on peaks?
   *Workers take time to get into their work. A warm-up period is needed.*

5 Why does the overtime period appear to be so safe?

*It may be because the maximum work period is 1.5 hours. On the other hand, it could be that there was very little overtime work during the period of the survey.*

## Target student commentary

This graph suggests that there are five accident peaks during the typical working day at A and G. The two smallest peaks seem to be connected to the period after clocking-on in the morning and afternoon. This may be due to the need for adjusting to the work environment after a long break. The next two peaks seem to occur just before tea breaks. They follow work periods longer than 1.25 hours and may indicate that fatigue sets in after that period. This and the approach of the break may cause lack of concentration and thus the accident peaks. The major peak of the day takes place at the end of normal working time between 4 and 5 p.m. This is possibly the result of a combination of a long, final work period and the approach of clocking-off. The safest periods of the day seem to be the 10.45 to midday period and the overtime period. Both these periods are divided into 1.25 hour sections. The figures for overtime, however, must be treated with caution. It may be that fewer accidents take place simply because little overtime work has been available. On the other hand, it could be that higher pay rates during overtime encourage more care and attention. Overall, this graph suggests that there may well be a case for reorganizing the working day.

---

# Page 6 Some educated guesses

Students study a bar chart. This chart shows the causes of the accident statistics they have just analyzed on page 5.

## Analysis of accidents chart

### Note

Each bar represents one hour of the day whereas the first graph was plotted in quarter hour periods. Each bar will therefore be higher than the respective plots in the first graph and this is reflected in the vertical axis figures.

## Language objectives

1 Discussing causes of accidents using appropriate lexis, e.g. *failure to, negligence, fatigue.*
2 Expressing the breakdown of statistical information into its components, e.g. *About 60% of the accidents in the daily peak were due to failure to follow procedures.*

## Target lexis

| | | |
|---|---|---|
| procedure | to prevent | breakdown |
| protective | to take a short cut | malfunction |
| defect | to take risks | maintenance |
| carelessness | to take precautions | to maintain |

## Answers to questions

2 **Negligence** means carelessness. Although you followed procedures and wore protective clothing, you were not careful enough in your job.
**Failure to follow procedures** means that you did not obey the rules for your particular job. Perhaps you took a short cut.
**Failure to wear protective clothing** means, for example, that you did not wear the gloves or helmet provided.
**Machine/system defects** are the mechanical breakdowns that prevent you working.
3 Negligence and failure to follow procedures are the most common cause of accidents.

## Further questions

1 What is the most important cause of accidents in the first hour of the day?
*Machine/system defects.*
2 What happens to the number of machine defects during the morning?
*They go down.*
3 What is the most common cause of accidents in the afternoons?
*Failure to follow procedures.*
4 What is the pattern of machine defects in the afternoon?
*They start high, fall during the afternoon and then rise again at the end of normal working hours.*

## Target student commentary

This bar chart breaks down the causes of accidents into four main categories. Negligence is an important cause of accidents during the periods just before breaks and afternoon clocking-off times. A possible cause of this may be fatigue. It is noted that it becomes a major cause during work periods over 1 hour 30 minutes in length. Failure to follow procedures becomes more important as the day progresses and is most important in the last hour of normal working. Fatigue and complacency may be factors here. Failure to wear protective clothing is a constant problem throughout the day, although it disappears as a problem during overtime. The final factor, machine defects, varies as a cause of accidents. It is important at the start of work both in the morning and afternoon but declines during those work periods. It rises again at the end of the day and becomes the most important cause of accidents during the overtime period. This suggests that machine maintenance is carried out only during work periods and not before work begins. There may be a case here for changing the maintenance work periods to ensure machines are in working order at the start of every work period.

# Page 7 From the horse's mouth

Students listen to three interviews with men involved in some of the accidents. Then, using the *Safety meeting notes* as a basis for discussion, they devise a series of recommendations to improve A and G's accident record.

## Recorded interviews

### Language objectives
1  Identifying cause and effect.
2  Drawing conclusions from verbal reports.

### Target lexis

| Interview 1 | Interview 2 | Interview 3 |
|---|---|---|
| to pay attention to | site | to break an arm |
| to concentrate | to overlook | mechanical hoist |
| to get tired | mates | to get stuck |
| to feed something into | unconscious | to free something |
| guard | to knock out | nasty |
| | | to break down |

See pages 79-80 of the *Student's Book* for the tapescript.

### Answers to questions
2  **Interview 1** - The man cut his thumb on a saw.
**Interview 2** - The man was hit on the head by a brick.
**Interview 3** - The man broke his arm in a hoist.
3  **Interview 1** - The man was not concentrating. His negligence was due partly to the length of the first work period.
**Interview 2** - The man was not wearing his helmet. It is easy to forget to do things during a long work day.

**Interview 3** - The man did not follow procedures when he was trying to free a brick. People often try to take short cuts when machines break down. In this case, machines seem to break down too often.

### Further questions
1  Why does the first man think the first shift is too long?
*Because by that time he needs a break and a cup of tea. This is probably why he was looking at his watch.*
2  Why does the third man think that maintenance should be carried out when he's not working?
*Because preventive maintenance, i.e. maintenance while the machine is not in use, will save time and prevent breakdowns. The present system only reacts to breakdowns once they have happened.*
3  Why won't the third man break his arm again?
*Because the shock of his accident will make him more careful in future.*

### Target student commentary

The three accidents seemed to be the result of human error. The victims got tired, lost concentration, forgot to protect themselves or took short cuts. But there were underlying factors which contributed to the accidents. Some of the shifts are too long. Machines break down too often. People forget to do things unless they are reminded about the dangers.

### Safety meeting: 20/10 Notes

These notes provide the structure for the discussion which leads to the devising of a series of recommendations.

**1 Work Organization**
**The problem:**
It seems from the graphs that the incidence of accidents increases after work periods longer than 1 hour 15 minutes. This may be due to fatigue and to loss of attention and concentration in work which may be monotonous. There is also a general increase in accidents during the day, reaching a peak in the hour before clocking-off time.
**Possible recommendations:**
1 hour 15 minutes seems to be the ideal work period. This suggests that a shorter standard working period should be introduced. The question is how to organize the day precisely. There are four hours available in the mornings and afternoons. One possibility is:

|———————| |———————| |———————|
1hr 20 mins     1hr 10 mins     1hr 10 mins
(with 2 x 10 min. breaks)

This increases break periods by five minutes but this may be acceptable if work quality improves and the accident rate falls. To overcome the end of afternoon peak it may make sense to make the last work period much shorter, e.g. 1hour, i.e.:

```
|————————|  |————————|  |————————|
  1hr 20mins      1hr 20 mins        1 hr
```
(with 2 x 10 min. breaks)

## 2 Maintenance shifts
**The problem:**
Machine defects are a constant source of accidents. They are particularly important at the start of the morning and afternoons. They also build up towards the end of the day. Mechanical problems seem to accumulate and are then dealt with only when the new work period begins.

**Possible recommendations:**
We know from the interviews that the maintenance people work the same hours as everyone else. It would make sense for them to work ahead of normal shifts and to initiate a programme of preventive maintenance, i.e. checking machines constantly and anticipating faults rather than reacting to them.

## 3 Supervision
**The problem:**
With so many accidents due to the failure to follow procedures or to wear protective clothing, it could be that there is inadequate supervision of the safety aspects of work.

**Possible recommendations:**
Supervisors are busy people. Perhaps one person on each site should have special responsibility for supervising the safety aspects of work.

## 4 Safety awareness
**The problem:**
On any one site the number of accidents will be few therefore without constant reminders or greater publicity, people will not be ready to spot possible danger. Complacency about safety is always a problem.

**Possible solutions:**
1 Publicize the facts about accidents at A and G. Use shock tactics, e.g. It could be you next time!
2 Train the workforce to spot and avoid danger, e.g. with special training sessions, video programmes. Reward good ideas.
3 Identify the most dangerous areas and put up warning signs.
4 Introduce sanctions, e.g. fines, temporary lay-off for failure to wear protective clothing.

## 5 General working environment and conditions
**The problems:**
The general industrial environment has a number of problems of a psychological nature built into it. Some of these are:
a) settling-in time.
b) concentration spans.
c) boredom thresholds.
d) work incentives and motivation.
a) may account for the start of work peaks whereas b) and c) may account for the need for shorter working periods. d) may be the main factor behind the high overtime safety standards.

**Possible recommendations:**
a) *Settling-in time:* There may be a case for special work preparation sessions in which the workforce gears itself up psychologically for work. The Japanese, for example, have exercise sessions and may meet In quality circles at the beginning of the day. Another possibility may be for every worker to be made responsible for checking tools and machinery at the beginning of each work session.
b) *Concentration spans:* Evidence suggests that concentration begins to flag after 1 hour 15 minutes. Work reorganization as above or variation of responsibilities may help to overcome this problem.
c) *Boredom thresholds:* These will vary from job to job but clearly job rotation may again help here.
d) *Work incentives:* The fact that the workforce is on overtime rates after 5 p.m. may help to reduce accidents, although the evidence is not conclusive from the survey. However, it is possible that financial incentives may help to reduce accidents, e.g. time bonuses for jobs completed safely, prizes for sites which can reduce accidents most noticeably.

# Unit 3  A tale of two Everests

## Synopsis

This unit is about leadership. *Part 1 The mountain* describes Chris Bonington's 1975 expedition to Mount Everest. *Part 2 The company* deals with the problems which Rupert Boswell faced as Chairman of a fictitious company called Everest Pumps. Overall, the unit contrasts different styles of leadership in a multiracial context. The unit ends with an analysis of leadership in the students' own working lives.

## Case objectives

1 Identifying the human qualities that led to failure in one case and success in the other.
2 Focussing on the special problems of leading multiracial groups.
3 Identifying and discussing the central conflict between concern for the wellbeing of people and concern for the production aims of the organization.
4 Using a *Managerial Grid* as a basis for discussing leadership in the students' own work environment.

## Overall language objectives

1 Practising extensive listening skills.
2 Acquiring and using lexis related to personnel management.
3 Discussing personnel problems within a particular organizational structure.

## Suggested preparation

As this unit focusses heavily on listening, students could be asked to listen to the description of Bonington's expedition and the interview with Boswell as homework prior to classroom discussion of the two cases, if this is practical.

As a warm-up activity, take some photos of famous men and women leaders into class and ask what kind of leaders these people are and what qualities would be common to all leaders, e.g. *courage, determination, charisma.* Then elicit the specific qualities needed to lead a mountaineering expedition and lead into the unit.

## Classroom management

This unit follows a case study approach throughout. As an extra activity at the end of the unit, a role play could be set up where Boswell questions and is questioned by a management consultant on the reasons for his company's failure and his own failure.

If the listening tasks are not used as preparatory homework, then the class could be split into two groups, with one group listening to the Bonington narrative and the other listening to the Boswell interview. The groups could then report back to each other on what they have heard and on what conclusions they have drawn about the leadership qualities displayed by both men.

---

# Page 8  1 The mountain

---

Students read the introduction to the first of the two stories and then study the organization structure of Chris Bonington's mountaineering expedition.

## Expedition organization chart

### Language objectives

1 Describing the structure of an organization in terms of function and hierarchy, e.g. *Bonington was in charge of overall strategy.*
2 Predicting and describing likely problems between the levels of the organization, e.g. *There was the possibility of friction between the British and Nepalese members of the expedition.*

### Target lexis

| | | |
|---|---|---|
| organigram | leader | to supervise |
| pyramid | to be responsible for | chain of command |
| level | to be in charge of | rivalry |
| hierarchy | to report to | position |
| 'them and us' mentality | | |

### Answers to questions

2 The leader is in charge of strategy, overall planning and decision-making. The lead climbers are responsible for achieving the expedition's target of reaching the top of the mountain. The role of the sherpas is to guide the expedition. The porters' function is to carry equipment to the base camp.
3 Bonington has over 500 people to lead through very difficult conditions. The lead climbers may be individualists and very ambitious. There may be rivalry within this group. There is the possibility of friction between the lead climbers and the sherpas due to cultural and language differences. There may be status problems between each level. Overall, there may be the potential for cultural, linguistic and perhaps racial frictions between the British and Nepalese members of the expedition.

## Further question

What can Bonington do to minimize problems within these groups and between the groups?
*He must first of all understand the problems and then lead by example. He must be a good communicator. He must win the trust of everyone below him. He must create a team spirit.*

---

# Page 9 Bonington's plan

---

Students study the plan of Bonington's expedition, listen to the story of the expedition as told on a radio programme and then analyze and discuss the reasons for the expedition's success.

## Great Achievements of the 20th Century radio programme

### Language objectives

1 Listening for and identifying major problems.
2 Listening for and deducing leadership qualities.
3 Summarizing reasons for success.

### Target lexis

| | | |
|---|---|---|
| to fail | recruitment | to allocate |
| to tackle | to familiarize | task |
| notorious | to acclimatize | shop floor mentality |
| modest | cooperative | to take precautions |
| sponsor | to appoint | to commemorate |
| resources | to respect | to coordinate |
| to take advantage | relationship | to lead from behind |
| logistics | to cement | team effort |
| bottleneck | ambitious | final assault |
| to weld | tension | reserve team |
| individualist | to demotivate | to claim a life |
| sensitive | prima donna | |

See page 80 of the *Student's Book* for the tapescript.

### Answers to questions

**3 Problems**
**Stage 1**: to raise finance, plan the logistics of the expedition and to recruit the team.
**Stage 2**: to familiarize and acclimatize the team, and to establish good relationships with everyone involved.
**Stage 3**: to establish base camp and to allocate tasks.
**Stage 4**: to select the lead team.
**Stage 5**: to break through the rock band.
**Stage 6**: to reach the summit.

## Further questions

1 What was the main task of the leader with regard to the 500 people in the expedition?
*To weld them into one team.*
2 Why was the visit to Tangbotje monastery important?
*Because it demonstrated respect for the Nepalese and their culture.*
3 Why did Bonington not select his lead team at an early stage?
*Because it would demotivate some and encourage 'prima donna' behaviour in others.*
4 How did Bonington reduce friction in the team?
*By delegating and not interfering in tactical decisions.*
5 Why did Bonington lead from behind?
*Because his job was strategic coordination.*
6 Why did the final success happen in an unexpected way?
*Because the reserve team saw an opportunity and took it.*
7 What was the postscript?
*Bonington let other teams try for the summit and one man died.*

## Answers to questions at the bottom of page 9

1 **Bonington's qualities**: sensitive, respectful, intelligent, sympathetic, team oriented, determined, cautious, bold, open, flexible, decisive, charismatic.
2 Bonington managed to weld a group of individuals into one team. He won the trust of the Nepalese by respecting their culture, delegating responsibility and treating them as equals. He avoided friction amongst the lead climbers by delegating responsibilities, concentrating on strategic issues and letting individuals make important tactical decisions. At the same time, he allowed them to criticize him and contribute to the decision-making process.

---

# Page 10 2 The company

---

Students read about the second Everest, Everest Pumps. They then study and discuss Everest's organization chart.

You may wish to indicate that a company is also a group of individuals which has targets to achieve. Hint that the object of the exercise is to compare this organization with another, i.e. Bonington's expedition. Ask students to read the background to the company and then check comprehension. Then lead onto the organization chart.

## Everest Pumps chart

### Language objectives

1 Describing the structure of an organization in terms of function and hierarchy, e.g. *The production manager reports to the Board of Directors and is responsible for all factory operations.*
2 Predicting and describing likely problems between the levels of the organization, e.g. *A potential problem area is conflict between the workers from the Asian community and the supervisors.*

### Target lexis

| | | |
|---|---|---|
| reporting lines | middle management | skilled |
| operative | to be in charge of | semi-skilled |
| workforce | to be responsible for | labourer |

### Answers to questions

2 The Board of Directors is responsible for overall strategy and decision-making. Managers have special responsibilities, e.g. R&D and production. They are in charge of implementing decisions made at board level and making the day-to-day decisions of their own departments. The Production Manager has several levels beneath him. He supervises 12 foremen who are in charge of 50 skilled machinists and fitters. These people operate the machines in the factory. Below them are 105 other semi-skilled and unskilled operatives who carry out various jobs from welding to labouring.

3 There could be the usual problems of any hierarchical structure. Communication lines are lengthy. There is the possibility of conflict between lower and higher levels due to this separation. There may also be status problems between the skilled and non-skilled levels. The additional factor here is the problem of cultural and nationality differences within the workforce. The fact that these are combined with the normal hierarchical divisions could be a source of considerable friction and conflict.

# Page 11 **Boswell's plan**

Students study the plans of Rupert Boswell, Everest's Chairman, for entering the Middle East market. They then listen to an interview in which Boswell describes the different stages and shows how things went wrong. Students then analyze and discuss the causes of failure in Everest's attempt to get into the new market. Finally, students can compare the qualities of Chris Bonington and Rupert Boswell as leaders in their different fields.

## Interview with Rupert Boswell

### Language objectives

1 Listening for and identifying major problems.
2 Listening for and deducing leadership qualities.
3 Summarizing reasons for failure.

### Target lexis

| | | |
|---|---|---|
| company shake-up | to blow your top | quality control |
| supply side | behind schedule | work study |
| restructuring | to sack someone | shop floor |
| demanning | out of the blue | to squabble |
| to tackle a problem | to insult | foul up |

See pages 81-82 of *Student's Book* for the tapescript.

### Answers to questions

**3 Problems**
**Stage 1**: to restructure the company financially, to reduce manpower, to buy new plant, to design new products and to find new markets.
**Stage 2**: to overcome personnel problems in the design department and to solve prototype problems.
**Stage 3**: to overcome personnel problems on the shop floor and to overcome a quality control problem.
**Stage 4**: to sort out problems of salesmen in the Middle East and to end a strike in the factory.
**Stage 5**: to negotiate a good price for the contract.
**Stage 6**: to close the deal.

### Further questions

1 What new market was Everest aiming at?
*The Middle East.*
2 What new product did Boswell want to manufacture?
*A pump that could withstand the worst Sahara sandstorm.*
3 How did Boswell show that he was in charge?
*He was firm and gave his staff bold, clear targets.*
4 How did Boswell solve the problem in the design department?
*He imposed a compromise and hired an outside consultant.*
5 What happened to the prototype?
*It broke down during dust tests.*
6 How did he solve the machinists' problem?
*He carpeted the personnel manager and foreman.*
7 What was the cause of the quality control problem?
*Half the machinists did not understand English.*
8 What caused the strike at the factory?
*The company refused to give the workers an hour off on a holy day.*
9 Why did Boswell fly out to the Middle East?
*To negotiate the final price.*
10 Why did Fawcett lose the contract?
*Because he did not have the power to make further concessions on price.*

## Answers to questions at the bottom of page 11

1 **Boswell's qualities**: tough, autocratic, single-minded, ruthless, insensitive, impulsive, egotistical, hard-nosed, aggressive.
2 He failed to win the respect and trust of his employees. Although he set clear targets, he set them without consulting his managers. He imposed decisions upon the company and acted in an autocratic and impulsive way. For this reason, he lost some good men and also caused the project to fall behind schedule. Although he is not racially prejudiced himself, he fails to help the victims of prejudice to overcome their problems. He is totally production oriented and shows a lack of interest in the human aspects of his company. He is also egotistical and finds it hard to delegate. He believes that only he knows best. His inability to let others make decisions finally caused Everest to lose the Middle East contract.

---

# Page 12 A question of leadership

From the *Managerial Grid*, students identify the different kinds of company leadership and decide how they would have handled Boswell's campaign.

## The Managerial Grid

This grid was first put forward by R. Blake and S. Moulton and attempts to show how different combinations of concern for people and concern for production may affect the success of a company. Moulton and Blake pointed out that the style of leadership often depends on the kind of company involved. For instance, service companies rely very much on personal commitment from staff and personal satisfaction from customers.

## Answers to questions

2 **1.9**
This kind of company needs commitment to efficient, dependable and continuous manufacturing. It therefore expects obedience from its workforce. The danger here is that autocratic leadership may cause resentment and demotivate people. High financial rewards may avoid this but in their absence conflict is likely to occur. Moulton and Blake refer to this as the *Authority/Obedience* style of management. Efficiency in operations ensures that human elements do not interfere in the smooth running of the business.

**5.5**
This style of management balances human needs with production needs. Here management consults its workforce in order to improve morale and encourage team orientation. At the same time it insists on strict production targets. Moulton and Blake refer to this as *Organization Man Management*. This is a balancing of the necessity to make people work with the maintenance of good company morale. It is often found in successful multinational manufacturing companies.

**1.1**
In this position there is hardly any management at all. The company may be running successfully at the moment, for example because it is a protected industry and there is a plentiful supply of labour. There is likely to be resentment and frustration among the workforce. The company will fail if it has to face the real competitive world. Moulton and Blake refer to this as *Impoverished Management*. Minimum effort by all concerned is sufficient to keep the organization going.

**9.1**
This kind of company focusses almost completely on the individual. It is likely to be a service industry where individual effort and commitment are vital and where the customer may respond personally to the service. Moulton and Blake refer to this as *Country Club Management*. Complete attention to peoples' needs and the encouragement of full, satisfying relationships lead to a comfortable, friendly organizational atmosphere and work tempo.

**9.9**
This style of management probably only occurs where everyone in the organization has a stake in its success. It is totally team oriented, and the commitment to the team and each individual in it coincides with maximum effort towards the production targets. Moulton and Blake refer to this as *Team Management*. Work is produced through committed people. Their interdependence through a common stake in an organization leads to relationships of trust and respect.

3 Bonington would be in the area of 8.7, i.e. his concern for people was high and coincided with the concern for results. His *Team Management* style was appropriate to such an expedition. Boswell would be in the area of 2.8, i.e. concern for production far exceeds concern for people. It is the *Authority/Obedience* style of management.
4 Points that should arise: delegation; cultural sensitivity; team spirit, especially among the sales force and design unit; consultation on the shop floor; flexibility in planning.

# *Pause for thought 1*

## A short course in leadership

### Synopsis
This unit provides the basis for a discussion of the qualities which make a good leader.

### Suggested exploitation
1 Allocate each phrase to a student or small group in the class and ask them to think of a situation where the use of this phrase would be appropriate. Ideally, the students could act out a situation for each phrase. Alternatively, ask each student or group to describe, orally or in written form, that situation which may be from their own experience or of their own invention.
2 Write the following list of words and phrases on the board or O.H.P. transparency and ask students to allocate them to the seven phrases on page 13.

| | |
|---|---|
| grateful | autocratic |
| polite | no one is infallible |
| respectful | to encourage |
| egotist | to consult |
| to motivate | team spirit |
| fair | to demotivate |
| to give credit where credit is due | to cooperate |
| sensitive | to involve |
| to show gratitude | to reward |

3 Check comprehension of words and ask students to make sentences using each of the words, e.g. *An autocratic leader can demotivate his staff.*
4 Ask students to describe managers they know or have known using the words above.
5 Ask students to draw up a character profile of the ideal manager for their own company, using the lexis above.

# Unit 4  New Formula Miracle

## Synopsis
This is a story of a product launch that goes wrong. Uniwhite, a detergent manufacturer, launches a new, improved version of its best-selling washing powder. The 'improvement' is an enzyme which causes skin complaints in a tiny minority of cases. These skin complaints are well-publicized in the media with the result that sales of the new product slump dramatically. Uniwhite has to decide how to react to the crisis.

## Case objectives
1 Describing the stages of a product launch.
2 Explaining and justifying a marketing strategy.
3 Analyzing the weaknesses in a marketing plan and devising plans to correct it.
4 Selecting the best way to overcome a major sales crisis in a fast-moving consumer goods market.

## Overall language objectives
1 Presenting new products.
2 Understanding and using the structures, functions and notions appropriate to the description of the history of a product.
3 Transferring information from the graphical-numerical medium to the verbal medium.
4 Taking part in the decision-making process in a meeting.

## Suggested preparation
Ask students to present products to each other using the language found in *Product and service presentation* on page x and then lead into the unit.

As preparatory homework, the students could be asked to prepare a presentation of the New Formula Miracle soap powder using the language in *Product and service presentation*.

## Classroom management
Once the scene has been set and the background information assimilated, this unit adopts a simulation approach. On page 16 students are asked to assume the roles of the main participants in the case. Students have to deal with two stages of the crisis. The first stage occurs on page 16 when the first newspaper article appears. Whatever decisions they reach at this stage should be assumed to be inadequate. The main pay-off to the case is the final stage of the crisis when a meeting is held at which the participants must decide on a plan of action to solve the problem. You may wish to allocate the roles

of Brand Manager, Marketing Director, Press and Public Relations Officer and Advertising and Promotions Manager to individual students right from the beginning of the unit.

To add further interest to the simulation, the role of the Uniwhite Chairman may be introduced in the final stage of the crisis. One of his or her targets should be to find out who is responsible for the crisis. The other participants will then have to defend their positions at the same time as presenting solutions.

Should you be short of time, pages 14 and 15 could be studied as preparatory homework. The simulation could then begin with Diane Sherrin's presentation of the newspaper report on page 16. The material on page 19 is optional.

---

# Page 14  New Formula Miracle

---

Students read the introduction to the company and the business situation, and then study and present the new product.

From the opening narrative, elicit the main reasons for the launch of an improved version of a successful product, i.e. *Market share of the original product was falling rapidly.*

## New formula Miracle pack

### Language objectives
1 Presenting and describing the features of a product, e.g. *New Formula Miracle contains a new ingredient called 'Bioboost'.*
2 Presenting and describing the benefits of a product, e.g. *The main benefit is its extra cleaning power at lower temperatures.*

### Target lexis
| | | |
|---|---|---|
| brand | packaging | benefit |
| brand name | size | advantage |
| manufacturer | slogan | selling point |
| trade mark | feature | ingredient |
| pack | | |

### Answers to questions
2 The main feature of the new product is the ingredient *Bioboost* which allows clothes to be washed at low temperatures. The major advantage

of this is that using colder water makes washing more economical. Uniwhite claims that the new powder will also make clothes cleaner and whiter than other products. Overall, the pack emphasizes the new formula and its advantages, although it does not specify what the new formula contains.

# Page 15
# Background: from hot washes to cold washes

Students familiarize themselves with the history of Miracle and the changes in washing machine technology. They then study the launch programme for New Formula Miracle and identify missing information on the chart. They supply that information by listening to a presentation by James Toft, Uniwhite's Marketing Director.

Ask students to read the background passage.

## Questions

1  How long has the Miracle brand been on the market?
   *10 years.*
2  What are the benefits of low temperature washes?
   *They are kinder to clothes and more economical.*
3  How much market share has Miracle lost in one year?
   *17%*
4  What share of the total market do enzyme powders now have?
   *30%*
5  Why did Uniwhite not use the word enzyme in the new powder?
   *Because enzymes had caused skin irritation problems in other brands.*

## New Formula Miracle launch programme

### Language objective

Listening for specific information.

### Target lexis

| | | |
|---|---|---|
| to test | advertising | follow-up |
| to approve | to discontinue | leaflet |
| to finalize | to start up | revised target |
| trade press | campaign | |

## Answers to questions

3  Consumer tests. Total number = 5,000.
   Positive = 97%. Negative = 3%.
   Enzyme content to be called *Bioboost*.
   Trade press advertising value = £2m.
   TV, press and radio campaign total value = £8m.
   End of year target brand share = 40%.
   Revised end of year target share = 50%.

See page 82 of the *Student's Book* for the tapescript.

# Page 16
# New Formula Miracle runs into trouble

Students find out what happened one month after the launch of New Formula Miracle. They read and report on a newspaper article which threatens the new product's prospects in the market place. They then devise a plan of action to deal with the threat.

## The big itch in your washing powder

### Language objectives

1  Inferring meaning from a headline, e.g. *The headline seems to suggest that a washing powder is causing discomfort among users.*
2  Skim reading for gist, e.g. *The general message is that some users of New Formula Miracle are complaining because it is causing skin problems.*
3  Reporting the content and bias of an article, e.g. *The article is critical of Uniwhite and hints that the company has not been frank with its customers.*

### Answers to questions

2  The article starts with a 'scare headline'. It then goes on to say that consumer groups have been getting complaints about the effects of New Formula Miracle on users' skins. It reports that these groups have been recommending those affected to switch to non-biological brands. According to the correspondent, the National Skin Council has just withdrawn its recommendation for Miracle. It says that its own tests show a high skin response to the new product. The article suggests that Uniwhite is being defensive about the product. Overall, it is a very damaging story.

3 Uniwhite could do various things at this stage, e.g. hold a press briefing to demonstrate the meticulous testing procedure used before the launch of New Formula Miracle; hold informal talks with the National Skin Council to reassure them; use advertising to reassure housewives.

### Possible courses of action arising from discussion
• There must be immediate action to limit the damage.
• A high profile response would be to hold a press conference and release results of the original tests. But this might attract more adverse press.
• A low key response would be background press briefings with sympathetic journalists and perhaps some 'letters to the editor' from contented users of New Formula Miracle. But this might not be enough.
• 'Wait and see' might be another option.
• Product changes are not necessary at this stage.

# Page 17 Crisis!

Students find out what happened over the next month. The information is contained in a graph used at a meeting on December 1st. The students study and report on this graph according to their particular roles. They then listen to the part of the meeting where Diane Sherrin presents her arguments.

## New Formula Miracle graph

### Language objectives
1 Presenting information on graphs verbally, e.g. *Sales of New Formula Miracle rose steeply during the month of October.* (See *Information presentation* on page vii in the *Language reference unit.*)
2 Using the simple past and present perfect tenses by identifying December 1st as NOW, e.g. *Sales increased during October but have fallen sharply since then.*
3 Expressing cause and effect, e.g. *The fall in sales revenue was the result of the adverse publicity in the press.*

### Target lexis

| | | |
|---|---|---|
| to phase out | dramatically | to reduce |
| revenue | suddenly | to be on target |
| to rise | to slump | to be on budget |
| to fall | to reach | to be over budget |
| to peak | to stand at | to be due to |
| steeply | to raise | to be the result of |

## Answers to questions
2 Original Miracle was phased out by week 41. Sales of the new product in the launch week were more than equal to the normal sales of Original Miracle. In the following weeks sales rose quickly from about £1.5m per week to around £2.4m a week in week 44. But in that week sales peaked out, as you can see, following the first newspaper article. In weeks 45 and 46 revenues fell significantly. There was an even more dramatic slump in week 47 and this is probably due to considerable media attention in that week. Since then, sales have continued to fall but at a slightly slower rate. This is probably a response to the increased advertising designed to counteract the bad publicity.
3 The advertising campaign started in early September and built up quickly during the fortnight before the launch. In the three weeks after the launch the advertising expenditure rose in line with budget to a peak of £1.4m. In week 43 the spending was reduced. In week 46, as a response to the market situation, it was decided to raise expenditure to counteract the bad publicity. This took us over budget but managed, I think, to slow down the rate of decline in sales.
4 The first newspaper article appeared in week 44 and was followed at the end of that week by another article. The first television coverage came in the next week. Week 46 was probably the worst week as far as press attention was concerned. It was probably responsible for the serious slump in sales. Since then, there has been only one further example of media attention although that was only four days ago. It could be that the storm has blown over!

## Listening to part of the discussion
### Language objectives
1 Listening for and summarizing the gist of an argument.
2 Listening for and identifying key meeting exponents, e.g. *All I'm saying is that ...*

### Target lexis

| | |
|---|---|
| to head off | suicide |
| thrill | skin response |
| human interest story | to devote (time) to |
| version | to pick on |
| environmentalists | to impress |
| to publish | to feel betrayed |

See page 82 of the *Student's Book* for the tapescript.

## Answers to questions

2 Sherrin argues that they should have published their lab test results long ago. Now it is too late and the press have a story which will not go away. She does not think that New Formula Miracle is more harmful than any other enzyme powder but the fact they have taken such a high profile has made Uniwhite an easy target.

---

# Pages 18 and 19

---

Students look at further information concerning the deteriorating market situation. The information is presented in the form of a brand switching graph. After this, they hold a meeting to devise a plan of action to save the situation.

You may wish to use the options on page 19 as a basis for the discussion but it is not necessary to do so. Students may well be able to devise their own options without reference to this text.

## Brand switching patterns: September-December

### Language objectives

1 Presenting information in a graph verbally, e.g. *Until week 44 New Formula Miracle took market share from Bril. Since then, Bril's market share has recovered and now exceeds Miracle's.*
2 Describing movement in the market, e.g. *The major impact of the launch of New Formula Miracle was on the non-biological Bril.*
3 Interpreting information, e.g. *This suggests that...*

### Target lexis

to switch from/to
pattern
trend
to try out
to respond to
to be squeezed
to be damaged by
to have an impact on

to take market share from
brand loyalty
at the expense of
to recover
to slump
to win back
to lose initial gains

### Answers to questions

2 Before the launch of New Formula Miracle, market shares were stable. Non-biological powders had about 60% of the market while biological powders had about 30%. Uniwhite's market share increased substantially after the launch of New Formula Miracle and rose to a peak of over 50% in week 44. This altered the balance between biological and non-biological powders dramatically. From a share of about 30% of the market in week 37, biological powders rose to almost 70% of the market in week 44. After the press publicity in week 44, however, Uniwhite's share fell and consumers switched to Maslow and Scotts' non-biological Bril. By week 46, market shares were moving back in favour of non-biological powders. By week 48, non-bio powders had recaptured lost ground and accounted for almost 50% of the market. Bril's share was now almost 40% compared with about 25% before the launch of New Formula Miracle.

3 One possible explanation is that a majority of consumers are traditionally unsure about enzyme powders because of earlier bad publicity or because of genuine skin complaints. Many of these switched to New Formula Miracle because of the massive advertising, its extra cleaning power and because it was not clear that Miracle had now become biological. When it became clear that it was a biological powder there was a massive reaction against Miracle. Bril users who had tried out Miracle returned to Bril together with the unhappy traditional users of Miracle. It should be noted that disappointed New Formula Miracle users did not switch to Uniwhite's other non-bio product Max. This may indicate a sense of anger towards Uniwhite. Overall, it may be that Uniwhite made a major error in introducing what amounted to a brand new product under the name of an established and relatively successful older product. It now has a brand problem, a product problem and a corporate image problem all wrapped up in one.

## Agenda

1 **Present market situation and forecasts:** This can be handled by the Marketing Director. He should use the sales revenue diagram and brand switching diagrams as bases for his forecasts, i.e. he must decide whether the situation will stabilize, get worse or improve.
2 **The media problem:** This can be handled by the PR officer.
3 **The sales, marketing and advertising problem:** This can be handled by the Brand Manager and Advertising Manager together.
4 **The product problem:** To be handled by the Brand Manager.
5 **Options open to Uniwhite:** Open discussion chaired by the Marketing Director. (*See page 19 for possible decisions.*)
6 As for 5.

# Possible outcome

1 Continue with the present strategy and assume that the adverse publicity will die down and that the tiny minority of customers with skin complaints will transfer to other powders. With continued advertising, customers will come back to New Formula Miracle because of its undoubted superior cleaning and whitening powers. This approach could be combined with an aggressive advertising campaign stressing the safety of New Formula Miracle. Against this are the facts that the market may not be ready for a major switch over to biological powders, that traditional users may feel betrayed and that the product may be permanently damaged in the market place by the publicity. As far as advertising is concerned, it may be better to let sleeping dogs lie!

2 Continue with the present strategy but admit there has been a problem with the product and change the enzyme to a milder kind even though this may mean a loss of cleaning and whitening power.

By announcing this to the press, the sting may be taken out of the adverse publicity. On the other hand, it may simply confirm the original bad publicity. Also, any admission of responsibility would probably lead to action in the courts by disaffected users.

3 Withdraw New Formula Miracle from the market and replace it with Original Miracle in a major advertising campaign designed to win back traditional users. The problem with this would be that it is essentially an admission of failure and even culpability.

4 Reintroduce Original Miracle to run alongside New Formula Miracle. With a carefully worded advertising campaign, it could be presented as a way of offering customers a complete range of powders for every need and every skin. It would avoid the problem of admission of failure or culpability.

**Note**

This case study is based on a real life situation. After suffering considerable losses, the company concerned opted for option 4 above. Several of the managers involved lost their jobs.

# *Pause for thought 2*

## Tinker, tailor, soldier, sailor...

### Synopsis

This unit is based on the National Readership Survey's breakdown of Britain's population in terms of socio-economic class. This breakdown is used by most advertising, sales and marketing organizations in the U.K. as a means of categorizing consumer groups and their behaviour. Although to some extent its categories coincide with income levels, it should be noted that job backgrounds, attitudes and cultural factors are equally important considerations in their categorization.

### Suggested exploitation

1 Ask students how people measure class differences in their own countries. Elicit income, wealth, job, ethnic background, education, culture, appearance, speech, manners.

2 Discuss how each of these factors might influence peoples' buying patterns, e.g. newspapers, clothes, holidays. Then lead the discussion onto the NRS categories. Check lexis and note the proportions for each class in the country as a whole. Note how these proportions have changed:
    i) very small fall in A households.
    ii) slight upward shift to B households.
    iii) stability in C1 households.
    iv) fall in C2 households.
    v) fall in D households.
    vi) large rise in E households.

3 Elicit reasons for changes, e.g. increased unemployment, changing job patterns due to mechanization of unskilled, semi-skilled jobs, increase in old age pensioners, rise in service industries and professions.

4 Allocate each class to individuals or small groups and ask them to describe a typical person or family in each class category. They may use knowledge from their own countries if appropriate or base their answers on the previous discussion. The students' final descriptions should include:
    i) relative income levels.
    ii) typical jobs.
    iii) political views.
    iv) attitudes to property, society, fashion, education, law and order, other classes and work.
    v) hobbies and interests.

5 End the discussion by asking students to talk about the desirability or inevitability of class systems either in the U.K. or their own countries, e.g. *What damage does the class system do? What good, if any, does a class system do?*

## Synopsis

Students analyze the range of British daily national newspapers in terms of content, political position, price and target readership with the aim of finding a gap in the market for a new newspaper which they then profile.

## Case objectives

1 Analyzing a market and breaking it down into clearly defined sectors.
2 Identifying potential gaps in a market.
3 Setting out clear marketing objectives for a particular product.
4 Devising a product and marketing plan to achieve the agreed objectives.

## Overall language objectives

1 Comparing and contrasting the features of different sectors of a market.
2 Expressing the quantitative aspects of a market.
3 Describing the qualitative aspects of a market.
4 Arguing a case for a particular new product development programme.
5 Presenting a marketing strategy for a new product.

## Suggested preparation

Ask students to study a selection of British newspapers, if this is possible, prior to analyzing the data in the unit. Any of the tasks on pages 21, 22 and 23 can be allocated as preparatory home study work, either to the whole class or to smaller groups or individuals for presentation in class.

## Classroom management

The unit is very flexible, and a number of different simulation approaches could be employed satisfactorily. The approach in the *Student's Book* is as follows:
Having analyzed the data on pages 21, 22 and 23, students are asked to take the role of a potential newspaper owner to decide what kind of newspaper they want. This role could be assigned from the beginning of the unit.

Alternatively, students could be asked, from the beginning of the unit, to take the roles of market researchers responsible for different areas of research. They would have to present their analysis of the market prior to a round-table discussion at which a profile of the new newspaper is worked out. This profile could then be presented to the potential owner. If you are short of time, the material and tasks on page 25 could be omitted.

## Page 21 Fleet Street

Students read the introduction to the unit, from which they should deduce that, owing to recent changes, there is now a better chance of making a profit on national newspapers than before. They then analyze the diagram.
**Note**
To do question 1, students must have access to British newspapers.

## Britain's national press diagram

It should be noted that this analysis is subjective in terms of left/right, light/serious analysis. You may wish to describe and position the newspapers in the diagram differently or to debate their positioning.

## Language objectives

1 Comparing and contrasting products in terms of quantity sold, e.g. *The Daily Telegraph's circulation is three times greater than The Guardian's, and in terms of position in the market, e.g. The Times is slightly to the right of centre compared with The Guardian which is to the left of centre.*
2 Expressing opinions about ways of breaking markets down into sectors, e.g. *In my view, the right of centre tabloid papers represent the largest single sector of the market.*
3 Identifying and describing opportunities in the market place, e.g. *There's a tremendous opportunity for a newspaper right in the middle of the market.*

## Target lexis

| | | |
|---|---|---|
| sector | editorial position | bias |
| segment | right wing | middle of the road |
| market position | left wing | readership |
| circulation | | |

## Answers to questions

2 Basically, the diagram suggests that there are four sectors to the market: left of centre serious; right of centre serious; left of centre light; right of centre light.
3 left of centre serious: 466,029
right of centre serious: 1,782,000
left of centre light: 3,505,000
right of centre light: 9,547,000

## Target student commentary

The British national press seems to be dominated by the popular newspapers with right of centre views. The total right of centre circulation is 11,329,000 compared with only 3,971,029 for left of centre papers. The serious press also seems to have a similar bias. Overall, the serious press accounts for a very small proportion of sales in terms of circulation. The diagram suggests that there is a gap in the market for a middle of the road, semi-serious newspaper.

# Page 22

Students study the contents of the three British newspapers and, if British newspapers are available, go on and analyze the contents of other British newspapers in the same way as in the diagram on the page.

## Britain's Dailies – the contents

### Note

It should be pointed out that this is necessarily a subjective and simplified breakdown of content on one day.

### Language objective

Analyzing, discussing and comparing diagramatic information.

### Target lexis

| | | |
|---|---|---|
| bar chart | source of revenue | element |
| segment | emphasis | mix |
| proportion | | |

### Answers to questions

2 They all have roughly the same proportion of advertising, i.e. between 33 and 43%.
3 *The Guardian* has a much greater emphasis on national and international news. *The Sun* and the *Daily Express*, concentrate on human interest stories. *The Sun* has a much greater proportion of pictures than the other two papers. Competitions also feature significantly in *The Sun* and to a lesser degree in the *Daily Express*.

### Further questions

1 What is the largest item of content for each newspaper?
*Advertising.*

2 Why is the advertising content so large as a proportion?
*Because it is an important source of income for the papers.*
3 Why are the human interest and picture components of *The Sun* so large ?
*Because the readers probably prefer these stories and this form of presentation to the lengthy news analysis of the serious papers.*

## Target student commentary

Advertising accounts for about a third of the contents of each of the papers, suggesting that it is a vital source of income for all of them. On editorial content, the papers differ widely. *The Sun* and the *Daily Express* give emphasis to human interest stories and they also have a large proportion of pictures. *The Guardian* emphasizes national and foreign news whereas the *Daily Express* features only small amounts of each and *The Sun* almost totally ignores these aspects of the news.

## Questions at the bottom of the page

1 and 2 Doing these tasks obviously depends on the availability of British newspapers. Question 2 previews the analysis on page 23.

# Page 23 Your daily paper – all is revealed!

Students analyze the two charts to build up a picture of the kinds of people who read the range of daily newspapers.
### Note
If students have copies of British newspapers available, then they can identify their newspaper on the two charts. If not, then they must study the information about the three newspapers described on page 22. Note also that the *Today* and *The Independent* newspapers are not included in these charts as figures were not available so soon after their launches.

## Who reads what?

### Language objectives

1 Interpreting and discussing the information contained in a numerical table, e.g. *78% of The Guardian's readership comes from the ABC1 status categories.*

2 Comparing and contrasting items within a table, e.g. *Compared with the Guardian, The Times has a higher proportion of readers in the A category – 15% against 7% – but a lower proportion in the C2 category – 9% against 13%.*

## Target lexis

| | | |
|---|---|---|
| table | category | to consist of |
| column | status | to comprise |
| percentage | profile | to break down |
| social class | to account for | |

## Answers to questions

2 **Example**: Almost 60% of *Times* readers come from the two upper social categories with a further 25% coming from the lower middle classes. The remaining 16% come from the C2DE categories.

## Does age make a difference?

Language objectives are as for the above chart.

## Target lexis

| | | |
|---|---|---|
| age group | middle age | over 65s |
| youth | elderly | age profile |
| pensioners | retired | to cater for |

## Answers to questions

3 **Example**: *The Daily Star* has the youngest readership of all the papers. 28% of its readers are under 25. It also has one of the smallest proportion of readers over 65. Between the ages of 25 and 65, however, its readership pattern follows the national age profile.

---

# Page 24 **Watch this space!**

---

Students should by now have a good idea of the sectors of the market and the kind of people who constitute the readership of the various newspapers. Students now bring together this information in order to devise a profitable newspaper of their own. First, they will decide what their motives and objectives are, e.g. influence, profitability, then they will build a target class, age and content profile of their new newspaper.

## Answers to questions

1 Possible objectives are: profit maximization; political influence; social status as owner; to inform and educate; to entertain; to correct a bias in the existing national press; to represent the interests of a particular group, e.g. trades unions. Various combinations of these are, of course, possible. Students may like to debate the 'proper role of a newspaper'.

2 Students should now begin to plan the best way to achieve their aims as decided above. They should start with the target sector most likely to expedite their aims, e.g. the mass market, right of centre tabloid sector if the aim is profit maximization. They should then go on to fill in the *Target reader* grid.

## 1 The target reader grid

### Details to be filled in

1 **Social class**: Clearly students will go for the C2DE sectors if maximum circulation and profit are needed. If political influence on government is required, they may target the AB groups. If they wish to correct a bias in the middle market range, they may appeal to the BC1 categories.

2 **Possible job**: On the basis of the social class decision made above students may refer to *Pause for thought 2* on page 20 in order to translate the categories into actual professions, e.g. C1 would consist of teachers, university students, bank clerks and clerical grade civil servants.

3 **Salary**: Students may do some research of their own here and find out in the most discreet way the salary of, for example, a typical teacher!

4 **Age group**: This will depend to some extent on the decisions made above. The point should be made that loyalty is a very strong sales factor in newspaper buying habits and therefore customers should be won over when they are young. However, if influence on decision makers is a target, then the 35-65 age group may be the main target here.

5 **Interests**: These should emerge through a discussion about the age, social status and job positions above, e.g. *What would be the interests of a typical DE 15-24 year old reader? Pop music, sport, etc.*

6 **Political position**: These may range from extreme left to extreme right but remember that neither of those positions seems to sell many newspapers. Remember also that an apolitical position may be appropriate in some cases.

7 **Present newspaper**: This should bring the discussion back to the target sector and the question of how to attract readers away from the competition, e.g. If the students have targeted the heavier popular sector they will have to design a newspaper that will draw readers away from the *Daily Mail* and the *Daily Express*.

## 2 The newspaper

Before filling in details students should carry out a detailed discussion about the contents and aims of the newspaper they are inventing. This discussion could be simply at the level of style, political bias, size, price and readership or it could include discussions of likely circulation forecasts, profit estimates and price sensitivity. Clearly, students following this unit as a project will spend more time on this section and expand it into the design of an actual newspaper.

**Name:** To be decided.

**Target circulation:** This should be at least 600,000. Students may also try to indicate from which competitive products this circulation may be captured, e.g. 10% from the *Daily Mail* readers, 20% from the *Daily Express*, 30% from new readers.

**Price:** See *The price of your news* on page 25. Students must take into account competitors' prices and the income levels of target readers.

**Political position:** Students should refer back to the chart on the first page of this unit.

**Special features:** Students should invent a component which would make their newspaper different from the competition and thus aid entry into a very difficult market, e.g. full colour pictures.

---

# Page 25 Some items of late news

---

Students find further information which may cause them to reconsider earlier decisions. First, they will see that some of the market gaps were once occupied by newspapers that failed to survive. Second, they will look at the prices of the current newspapers. These will help business students to calculate potential turnover and profit figures.

## The newspapers that lived and died

### Answers to questions

2 The collapse of two left of centre papers may mean that the market for such a politically positioned paper is limited, particularly towards the heavier popular and serious end of the market. Owners wishing to correct a bias in the existing press may have to attack the *Mirror's* niche head on. Also, a more middle market tabloid may run into difficulties if this area of the market is limited.

### Target student commentary

The existing gaps in the market may not be gaps at all. These positions were once occupied by newspapers that went out of business. The reasons for this are not clear. If the failures were due to bad management, then the market positions may be open. If demand trends moved away from these positions, then sales potential may not exist.

## The price of your news

### Answers to questions

2 Students should make sure that the price they have decided for their newspaper is competitive. They may wish to adjust it downwards if a competitor is below them or at the same level. You may need to update this information.

## Possible outcome based on various target objectives

Students will probably target particular sectors of the diagram on page 21 according to the motives they decide to adopt in their roles as newspaper proprietors. The following are some examples of possible combinations of motive and sector targets :

1 **Profit maximization:** The most likely target here is the popular sector. This could be the heavier popular sector, or the lighter popular sector.

2 **Status and political influence:** The most likely target here would be the quality sector. The teacher may point out that *The Independent* was launched in 1986 in this sector and has so far proved very successful.

3 **Bias correction, profit, informing motive:** This may cause students to target the apparent gap in the market, i.e. the large central area between serious and light, left and right. *The Today* newspaper launched in 1986 approached this zone.

# Unit 6 Adventure Holidays International

## Synopsis

Adventure Holidays International offers holidays which combine history, culture and adventure. Its most popular holiday is in a North African country where holidaymakers take part in staged activities such as raids and palace coups. These activities quite understandably offend the government of the country and AHI now has to decide how to deal with the resulting threat to its main business.

## Case objectives

1 Identifying and discussing the problems created by selling services on the basis of customers' misconceptions and prejudices about the real world.
2 Discussing the political and moral implications of such a sales and advertising policy.
3 Deciding how to handle an immediate crisis involving a company's representatives and image in a host country.
4 Devising a suitable long-term strategy to overcome the present problem and to prevent its recurrence.

## Overall language objectives

1 Analyzing the language of advertising.
2 Interpreting statistical information.
3 Taking part in a meeting to decide on a course of action.

## Suggested preparation

Ask students to listen to the radio advertisement, if this is possible, and read the Saladdin advertisement on page 26 as preparatory homework. As a warm-up activity, ask students about their own holiday experiences, e.g. *What kind of activities do you like to do? Do you think there has been a change in what people expect from a holiday? What new kinds of holidays are available?*

## Classroom management

This unit adopts a case study approach until the last activity on page 29 where students are asked to take part in an AHI board meeting to discuss and decide on a plan of action in the face of the crisis. Pages 26 and 27 contain important background information to the crisis which comes on page 28.

## Page 26
## A recipe for success

Students read the introductory text, listen to a radio commercial and read an advertisement. From the introductory text establish why AHI's holidays are different and the fact that there is a new sister company operating in the Middle East.

## Radio advertisement

### Language objectives

1 Listening for specific information.
2 Talking about the psychology behind an advertisement.

### Target lexis

| | | |
|---|---|---|
| to set the scene | message | to appeal to |
| mood music | to specialize in | to attract |
| sound effects | experience | to involve |
| jingle | to persuade | |

See page 82 of the *Student's Book* for the tapescript.

### Answers to questions

2 It would probably appeal to young, adventurous people with a high level of income, e.g. young professionals.

### Target student commentary

This advertisement is trying to persuade the young, professional holidaymaker to buy a different kind of holiday. AHI's adventure itineraries involve exotic journeys based on actual historical events. These are followed by lengthy celebrations where the emphasis is on pleasure rather than adventure.

## Saladdin advertisement

### Language objectives

1 Reading for specific information.
2 Reporting on the contents of a text.

### Answers to questions

2 The itinerary begins at an oasis where the holidaymakers receive their personal camels. After this, they travel across desert, visit the Kharoumi caves and are raided by the Wakhoubi tribe. Following this, they climb the

Maraba mountains and then descend to a sultan's palace on the Mediterranean.

## Target student commentary

This advertisement combines history, culture and adventure in an attempt to attract the young holidaymaker who wants a holiday with a difference. The itinerary includes a five day desert journey, various events and visits to places of interest. It ends with eight days of palace life where the emphasis is on pleasure.

# Page 2  AHI – the best year yet

Students study the range of holidays available from AHI and MEH and then analyze the present booking situation for these two companies.

## AHI/MEH map and booking table

### Language objectives

1 Interpreting statistical information, e.g. *Saladdin is almost fully booked whereas Alexander has had only a few bookings so far.*
2 Comparing different products, e.g. *The holiday range goes from a short adventure holiday in Spain for £350 to the month long Alexander itinerary at £1,050.*

### Target lexis

| | | |
|---|---|---|
| itinerary | popular | to transfer |
| route | to comprise | place |
| product range | to reserve | unfilled capacity |
| value for money | overbooked | fully booked |

### Answers to questions

2 The immediate booking situation, i.e. for May, is as follows:
*Saladdin is almost fully booked while Caesar and Isobel have considerable capacity remaining. Alexander does not seem to have taken off yet. Almost 80% of MEH places have already been sold.*
3 In May there is a total of 100 spare places on the Isobel, Caesar and Alexander routes and only five places on the Saladdin route. There are still 85 places available on MEH holidays. (Students may make similar calculations for the following months.)

## Target student commentary

AHI's most popular itinerary is Saladdin. In the next two months it is fully booked and in July it is actually overbooked. The Caesar and Isobel itineraries are quite well booked, although there is still spare capacity on both of them. Last minute bookings, however, will possibly fill the spare places. The weakest product so far is Alexander.

# Page 28  Crisis!

Students read a newspaper article about an important political decision in Afaria and decide what action AHI should take in the light of it.

## Afaria clamps down on cultural exploitation

### Language objectives

1 Scanning a text for specific information.
2 Making suggestions to solve a problem.

### Target lexis

| | | |
|---|---|---|
| to exploit | degrading | to perform |
| to distort | humiliating | to claim |
| tradition | to ban | inaccuracy |
| belief | to offend | to boycott |

### Answers to questions

2 AHI is in danger of losing its most successful itinerary. Also , it looks like one of its local representatives has been arrested.
3 **Suggestion 1:** AHI should clarify the situation, e.g. *Has AHI been banned already or can it modify its itinerary to meet the new laws?*
   **Suggestion 2:** AHI should prepare a list of modifications which it can present to the government as concessions.
   **Suggestion 3:** AHI should draw up contingency plans to rescue customers already in the desert.
   **Suggestion 4:** AHI should draw up contingency plans to divert existing Saladdin bookings to other itineraries.

### Further questions

1 What does the government of Afaria object to? *Foreigners exploiting its people and culture and presenting an incorrect view of its past.*

2 What words does the Minister of Culture use
to describe the activities of the foreign
companies?
*Humiliating, degrading, cultural pornography.*
3 What will the government do to guilty companies?
*It will ban them.*
4 What other action might the government take
with its neighbours?
*It might ask for a boycott of the offending
companies.*

## Target student commentary

AHI is clearly in trouble in Afaria, although the
situation is still not completely clear. The new
government action obviously threatens not only AHI's
operations in Afaria but also its whole range of
business. Firstly, it may have to cancel all bookings to
that country or at least switch them to other
intineraries. Secondly it will receive damaging publicity
in the press, and, thirdly, any boycott in this part of the
world would be a disaster.

# Page 29
# The last letter from Afaria

Students read a letter from AHI's representative in
Afaria and then hold a meeting as members of the
AHI board to decide on the measures to be taken.

## The letter

### Language objectives

1 Scanning a text for specific information.
2 Summarizing the contents of a text.

### Answers to questions

2 Harding believes that the government is
trying to control the internal situation by
making concessions to the religious and ethnic
parties. Nevertheless, its main concern is
still the economy. For this reason they should
not believe everything they read or hear.
3 It is possible that the new measures are for
home consumption only and that in reality the
government will turn a blind eye to AHI's
activities. On the other hand, the government
may have chosen AHI as an example to
distract people's attention from larger foreign
companies operating in the country. At the moment
AHI has no alternative but to take the reports
seriously.

## Further questions

1 What concessions has the government made?
*It has given a cabinet seat to one of the
religious leaders.*
2 How might the competitor across the border
help AHI?
*AHI could switch some of its customers to
them if the situation got worse.*

## Target student commentary

Harding is clearly aware of the political problems in
Afaria and knows that the government has to
reconcile two conflicting interests. The first is to satisfy
the religious and ethnic forces in society and the
second is to ensure an improvement in the country's
economic performance. He believes that the latter is
still the government's main aim but that it will have to
pay lip service to the religious and ethnic forces. The
letter was sent before the new measures and it seems
possible that Harding has become a victim of a
government manoeuvre and been arrested.

# Agenda

## Language objective

Taking part in a meeting with the intention of solving a
crisis.

## Likely outcome

1 **Clarification:** What is really happening in Afaria? Is
there a possibility of changing the content of the
itinerary and avoiding a ban or has AHI become a
convenient scapegoat for the government? Is Harding
in prison and, if so, can he be released?
2 **Possible concessions:** If a ban is not certain,
what concessions can AHI make in the content of its
Saladdin itinerary without losing the customer appeal
that made it their best-selling route? For example, can
it change the ads, take out the raid and palace coup
elements?
3 **Impact of ban:** If a ban cannot be avoided, how
can AHI limit the damage to its business? How can it
rescue the groups now in the desert? Can it switch
customers to the other adventure itineraries? Can it
switch customers to the MEH locations? Can it
transfer customers across the border by doing a deal
with Experience Unlimited?
4 **Impact of boycott:** What action can AHI take to
avoid a total boycott in the region which would
probably have particular effects on MEH holidays in
the Middle East locations?
5 **Long-term policy:** What should be AHI's long-term
policy to make sure that this sort of problem does not
arise again?

**6 Action:** Students, first of all, should decide to clarify the situation. After that, they should prepare contingency plans to deal with the two main possible eventualities, firstly, that the government is still willing to negotiate and, secondly, that the government is making an example of AHI and that the ban is irreversible.

**Contingency 1 Negotiation:** AHI may be willing to omit particularly offensive activities from their itinerary, e.g. the raid and the palace coups and conspiracies. On the other hand, the government may be content if no mention of such activities is made in the AHI publicity materials. AHI could perhaps point to the income that the company brings to Afaria. AHI must be sure, however, that any changes to its product do not result in a fall-off in demand. More emphasis perhaps could be put on the physical aspects of the adventure rather than the fantasy element.

**Contingency 2 Outright ban:** In this situation AHI must (a) seek the release of Harding, (b) rescue customers now in Afaria, (c) keep as many bookings as possible by offering alternative itineraries, (d) avoid the wider boycott if possible, (e) limit the adverse publicity from the overall situation.

The company is in a weak bargaining position as far as (a) is concerned and will probably concentrate on (c).

It may: i) offer alternative itineraries at the same price. The problem here is that there are only 220 free places for the 345 bookings for Saladdin in May and June. The trouble with this is that each itinerary is of a different length. They could offer some of the MEH holidays also but they may not appeal to the adventure seeking customers of AHI. There is no doubt the company would make considerable losses here anyway.

ii) offer full refunds on all Saladdin bookings as a gesture of goodwill but in the hope that customers will transfer to other itineraries.

iii) offer an alternative but similar location for Saladdin.

iv) offer a holiday with Experience Unlimited.

v) offer places at similar prices and durations on other adventure holidays by increasing capacity on them.

# Suggested further activity: simulation

Divide the students into two negotiating groups a) the government of Afaria and b) AHI management. Ask the latter to negotiate with Afaria on all outstanding points to try and reach a deal.

## Suggestions

### AHI

1 Importance of AHI to the Afarian economy.
2 The possibility of reaching a compromise regarding the content of the Saladdin itinerary.
3 The possibility of emphasizing those aspects of Afarian culture that Afaria considers the most important.

### Afaria

1 The lack of importance of AHI to the Afarian economy.
2 The trivialization of Afarian culture through AHI publicity materials.
3 The offensiveness of AHI activities to the people of Afaria, e.g. raids, coups.
4 The willingness to ban AHI immediately.
5 The possibility of a wider regional boycott.
6 Appropriate concessions from AHI.

# *Unit 7* Yamacom

## Synopsis

This unit looks at what can go wrong when the human, cross-cultural aspects of an international business alliance are ignored. An American telecommunications company and a Japanese computer manufacturer merge and find that their employees do not work well together in the Indonesian office where the American manager, Paul Mackowitz, fails to get the cooperation of his Japanese staff. The Regional Director, Mark Weinberg, calls in an expert to study the problem and, then, on the basis of what he has learned, has to select a suitable candidate to replace the manager in Indonesia.

## Case objectives

1 Identifying and discussing some of the differences between Western and Japanese approaches to business.
2 Identifying some of the problems which may arise due to a lack of cross-cultural sensitivity.
3 Selecting a manager from a short list of four candidates.

## Overall language objectives

1 Interpreting diagrammatic information.
2 Using the appropriate language in a discussion of personal characteristics in a management context.
3 Taking part in recruitment discussions.

## Suggested preparation

Ask students to study the advertisement on page 30 prior to an introductory discussion on the question *Why do some marriages succeed and others fail?* Discuss the problems of personality clashes, different backgrounds, different tastes, and, hopefully, reach the conclusion that partners have to learn to adapt to each other. Then lead into page 31.

## Classroom management

This unit falls naturally into two stages: *Stage 1* is a study of the background to the merger, the specific problem in the Jakarta office and the general problem of cross-cultural integration, (pages 30 and 31). *Stage 2* is the task of choosing someone for the Jakarta job (pages 32, 33, 34 and 35). This unit follows a case study approach throughout, although in Stage 2 a simulation approach could be adopted with students taking the roles of interviewers and interviewees.

## Page 30 **A marriage is announced**

Students look at a map which shows the background and benefits of a merger between an American and a Japanese company.

## Yamacom: A New Force in TransPacific Cooperation

### Language objective

Interpreting and discussing diagrammatic information.

### Target lexis

| | | |
|---|---|---|
| to merge | advantage | culture clash |
| merger | synergy | language barrier |
| to integrate | hardware | to harmonize |
| to benefit from | know-how | to standardize |
| mutual benefit | | |

### Note

IT means information technology. This is an umbrella term for the industry behind the high speed processing and transmission of data and information, i.e. computers, satellites, and telecommunications.

### Answers to questions

2 The advantages for Transcom are entry to the Far East market, expansion into computers and a comprehensive IT product.
3 The advantages for Yamahata are entry to the U.S. market, expansion into telecommunications and a comprehensive IT product.

### Target student commentary

The overall advantage of the merger is the creation of a major global IT company with assembly sites and sales offices all around the Pacific basin. Both companies will gain entry into new markets and new technologies. The transfer of personnel will help to integrate the companies at an individual level.

# Page 31  A people problem

Students read about the situation one year later in Yamacom's Far East markets. Problems have emerged. The centre of these problems is in the Jakarta office. Mark Weinberg, Yamacom's Regional Director, overhears a conversation during a visit there. After this, the company asks an expert in cross-cultural communication to speak at a seminar about the differences between Western and Japanese business cultures.

## Conversation between Mackowitz and Watanabe

### Language objectives

1 Listening for and reporting the gist of a conversation, e.g. *They discussed the reasons why Mackowitz had sacked a man called Shigeta.*
2 Identifying the underlying behavioural aspects of a conversation, e.g. *Mackowitz is impatient with his Japanese staff.*

### Target lexis

| | | |
|---|---|---|
| angry | procedure | efficient |
| frustrated | contact report | hassle |
| insensitive | zap | attitude |
| impatient | to displease | to report back |
| to waste time | to get blood out of a stone | |

See page 83 of the *Student's Book* for the tapescript.

### Answers to questions

2 Shigeta was sacked because he did not follow the correct reporting procedures.
3 Mackowitz was impatient, individualistic and competitive while his Japanese colleagues looked for more personal contact and support, and took a more relaxed and longer-term attitude to following up sales leads.

### Further questions

1 Why did Shigeta not use a contact report?
   *There were no such procedures in Yamahata and everything was done at a personal and informal level.*
2 Why did Shigeta not explain this to Mackowitz?
   *Because he did not want to displease him.*
3 How did Shigeta waste time according to Mackowitz?
   *By always coming to his office instead of using the phone.*

### Target student commentary

Mackowitz is clearly used to working in an individualistic and competitive business situation where everything is highly systematized and pressurized. His Japanese colleagues are used to a slower, face-to-face business approach with the emphasis on personal relationships rather than business systems.

## Contrasts in Culture, Tradition and Behaviour

### Language objectives

1 Using the lexis appropriate to a discussion of national and cultural differences, e.g. *collective, individualistic.*
2 Expanding notes into full sentences or paragraphs in the context of a comparative analysis, e.g. *Westerners are encouraged to be independent and individualistic while the Japanese encourage dependent and collective attitudes.*

### Answers to questions

2 Mackowitz clearly saw Shigeta as incompetent. He is an individualist who believes in confrontation as a way of solving personnel problems. He wants independent initiative and efficiency from his staff.
3 Shigeta was afraid to explain his problems to Mackowitz because of his fear of shame. Both Japanese employees were used to cooperation and participation rather than Mackowitz's authoritarian approach to decision-making.

### Target student commentary

There are large differences between Western and Japanese culture and tradition which must affect the business process. The main difference is that the Western style emphasizes the importance of the individual in a competitive system while the Japanese style stresses the importance of cooperation within a collective system.

## The expert answers questions

### Language objectives

1 Notetaking important points from talks.
2 Writing a list of tips.

## Target lexis

| | | |
|---|---|---|
| to bridge a gap | to chop up | to value |
| precondition | organic | sentiment |
| mutual respect | to give a tip (hint) | crucial |
| sensitivity | patient (adj.) | embarrassment |
| culture | sincere | concessions |
| the small gesture | to take responsibility for | |

See page 83 of the *Student's Book* for the tapescript.

## Answers to questions

2 Be patient. Build up personal relationships. Don't hurry things. Remember the importance of gifts and entertainment. Don't be afraid of silences.
3 Be prepared for demands for quick decisions. Remember that Westerners separate their personal lives and feelings from their business lives. The person you meet in a business situation may be very different in a private situation. Apparent coldness or rudeness may be only an expression of efficiency. Be prepared for the attitude that it is the business that is important and not the people in it.

## Further questions

1 What are the expert's three conditions for success in foreign cultures?
   *Mutual respect, sensitivity, understanding.*
2 How much longer do negotiations in Japan take compared to the U.S.?
   *Six times as long.*
3 Why are expensive gifts not necessary in Japan?
   *Because gifts are valued for sentiment rather than money value.*
4 How has silence led to unnecessary concessions by business people visiting Japan?
   *Because Westerners felt they had to keep the conversation going.*

---

# Pages 32, 33 and 34
# A new beginning in Jakarta

---

Students learn that Weinberg decided to replace Mackowitz and then read an internal notice advertising the vacant Jakarta post. They then have to study the c.v.'s of the four short-listed candidates prior to the selection process on page 35.

As a warm-up to the study of the c.v.'s, students should discuss as a class or in small groups the qualities they should be looking for in a candidate. This can be done by looking ahead to the *Interview Assessment Summary grid* on page 35 and by asking questions like *What kind of background should the ideal candidate have?* and *What are the main*

personal qualities that the ideal candidate should have?

At this point, you may wish to adopt a simulation approach. If this approach is adopted, then some preparatory language work on conducting and taking part in interviews will probably be necessary.

**Note**

There are no tasks on the *Student's Book* page for this section of the unit.

## Yamacom position vacant notice

### Questions

1 What are the four major duties of the Jakarta position?
   *Administration, finance, sales, staff integration.*
2 Who is the immediate superior to the General Manager?
   *South East Asia Divisional Director Mr. Lee Than Quo.*

### Target student commentary

The Jakarta position involves full responsibility for the overall operation and performance of Yamacom Indonesia. The multinational character of this subsidiary will require somebody with excellent managerial and leadership skills in a multicultural context.

## CV 1  Thomas Jackson

### Questions

1 What is Jackson's academic background?
   *He has a degree in economics from Yale and a Harvard MBA.*
2 How long has he been with the company?
   *Five years.*
3 What did he do before he joined Transcom?
   *He was a salesman in fast-moving consumer goods.*
4 What are his major achievements so far in Transcom?
   *He expanded software packages for realtors to $50m.*
5 What aspects of his record and character would make him suitable for the Jakarta job?
   *He is committed to the company, is dynamic, successful and has lots of sales experience. He is also ambitious.*
6 What aspects of his record and character would make him unsuitable for the job?
   *He has no overseas experience, he is, perhaps, too individualistic, very American in his approach and demonstrates few interests outside a strictly American context.*

## Target student commentary

Thomas Jackson has an excellent record of achievement inside Transcom in the U.S. He is clearly an energetic, efficient and achievement-oriented individual with a lot of ambition. But his experience outside the U.S. is non-existent and his cultural involvements in sports and religion are restricted to his own country. His interest in the Jakarta position seems to be motivated by his own need for advancement in a company which has become international.

## CV 2  Stephanie Martinez

### Questions

1  How long has Martinez been with Transcom?
   *Two years.*
2  Why is she applying for the Jakarta job?
   *Because the Taipeh office is being closed down.*
3  What aspects of her record and character would make her suitable for the job?
   *She has worked in the Far East for four years, has been married to a Japanese and speaks Japanese.*
4  What aspects of her record and character would make her unsuitable for the job?
   *She has little sales experience and her time in the business world is limited. Also, her period in any one occupation seems to be limited to two years. Her wide range of interests may also point to a lack of genuine interest in business activities.*

### Target student commentary

Martinez is clearly a very bright and culturally sensitive person, and no doubt gets on well with people of different cultures from her own. However, her record may suggest a lack of 'sticking power' in any one area, position or occupation. Her interests also seem to be mainly in the academic and cultural areas, and it could be that she is using business as a passport to pursuing her real interests. These reservations could only be investigated by careful interviewing.

## CV 3  Lee Miller

### Questions

1  How long has Miller been with Transcom?
   *14 years.*
2  What aspects of his record and character would make him suitable for the Jakarta job?
   *He is from the Far East and yet has become an American citizen. He has served in the Far East and has an excellent record in his area of expertise both on the sales and technical side.*

## Target student commentary

Miller is at first glance a good candidate for this position since he is already bi-cultural in upbringing and experience. He also has a good track record on the work experience side. There is a suspicion of personal instability at different times in his life, e.g. the car crash and the divorce.

## CV 4  Dan Masters

### Questions

1  How long has Masters been with Transcom?
   *10 years.*
2  What aspects of his record and character would make him suitable for the Jakarta job?
   *He is obviously culturally sensitive and able to adapt to life overseas. He has an excellent record in sales management and also displays good leadership qualities. His interests indicate a broad personality.*
3  What aspects of his record and character would make him unsuitable for the Jakarta job?
   *He is clearly a man of principle and this may cause problems with superiors. He obviously has a reputation for making his own decisions.*

### Target student commentary

Masters is his own man. He knows where he stands on most subjects but he also has a very wide range of interests and abilities. His quiet approach to things and his knowledge of languages suggests that he would adapt well to a multicultural environment. But there is a question mark about his relationships with superiors.

---

# Page 35
# Final selection board

---

Students discuss the four candidates, score each of them on the *Interview Assessment Summary* grid and then, in groups, negotiate to select a final candidate.

### Language objectives

1  Assessing, comparing and discussing the suitability of candidates, e.g. *I think that Martinez has a lot of energy and enthusiasm but not as much experience as the others.*
2  Making a final decision and justifying that decision, e.g. *We have selected Dan Masters because of his combination of cultural sensitivity and proven track record.*

## Possible outcome

**Jackson** is clearly a dynamic, 'go-getting' American with no experience outside the U.S. It is likely that he would have similar problems in Jakarta to Mackowitz.

**Martinez** has good cross-cultural experience but does not seem to have held down a job for longer than two years.

**Miller** has an excellent track record and has adapted well to the European environment.

**Masters** is the most likely candidate. He has headed Transcom overseas sales offices for over three years and displays a broad personality and sensitivity to foreign cultures. Since he is his own man, he will probably stand a good chance of establishing a stable and effective operation in the Jakarta office.

# One man's view of
# European law

## Synopsis
This unit is a light-hearted look at national stereotypes which should be handled with sensitivity and tact.

## Suggested exploitation
1 Ask students to identify the main national characteristic that each extract suggests, e.g. *The Germans are strict. The French are permissive. The Soviet Union is repressive and the Italians are libertarian.*
2 Write the following list on the board and ask students to put the words or phrases against a suitable list of nationalities:

| | | |
|---|---|---|
| conservative | imaginative | kind |
| reserved | unimaginative | friendly |
| hard-working | repressive | unfriendly |
| lazy | formal | cold |
| logical | relaxed | warm |
| disciplined | humourless | hospitable |
| unruly | strict | illogical |
| respectful | disorganized | passionate |
| disrespectful | repressed | fair |

3 Discuss the lists on the board and ask people to justify, defend or attack the stereotypes suggested.
4 End the unit by asking students to think up reasons why national stereotypes are at best misleading and at worst dangerous.

# Unit 8 Oxfam

## Synopsis

Oxfam is faced by a sudden famine crisis in Ethiopia. It has to allocate a fund of £4m to the famine victims in its three feeding centres there. Students have to identify needs and priorities, and then make some very difficult decisions in allocating the £4m budget. There is a considerable amount of numerical work involved in this unit.

## Case objectives

1 Involving students in the problems of allocating limited funds to unlimited needs.
2 Analyzing needs and working out the priorities.
3 Devising the most cost effective method of satisfying need and achieving the overall targets of the operation.

**Note**

Oxfam's overall target is to save as many lives as possible. To do this they have to make sure that every penny is spent in the best way possible. To this extent, the processes involved in this unit are similar to any business budgeting, cost-controlling situation.

## Overall language objectives

1 Describing items of supply in terms of function and price.
2 Describing methods of distribution and transportation in terms of time, price and quality.
3 Negotiating and justifying the allocation of resources.

## Suggested preparation

Page 37 provides the introductory information to this unit and it could be given as preparatory homework.

## Classroom management

This unit adopts a case approach until page 41 where students are asked to take roles in the Emergency Unit. Students could be asked to take roles on pages 38 and 39, and make presentations, as members of the Emergency Unit, of the information on those two pages.

---

## Page 37 Oxfam

---

Students listen to a radio news item and study a map with text.

## The news that shocked the world

### Language objective

Listening to a news item and reporting back its content.

### Target lexis

| | | |
|---|---|---|
| famine | desperate | treatment |
| to starve | exhausted | shelter |
| barren | freak | drought |
| critical | crops | |

See page 83 of the *Student's Book* for the tapescript.

### Answers to questions

2 There is a famine in Ethiopia. 10,000 people have already died. In the camp mentioned there are already 50,000 people and more are still arriving.
3 The people at most risk are children, pregnant women and the old.

### Further questions

1 When did it last rain?
*Six weeks ago.*
2 What was the effect of the rain?
*It destroyed the remaining crops.*
3 What four kinds of help does the Oxfam director need immediately?
*Food, shelter, water and medical aid.*

### Target student commentary

The situation in the Oxfam camp is worsening. There are 50,000 people there already but more are arriving all the time. Food and other resources are needed.

## The famine in Ethiopia map

### Language objectives

1 Describing geographical location and supply routes, e.g. *The three camps are half way between Addis Ababa and Assab.*
2 Describing journey times and distances, e.g. *It takes 30 days from the U.K. to Assab by sea.*
3 Describing categories of need, e.g. *The most urgent needs are those of the severely malnourished.*

### Answers to questions

1 One method is by sea from the U.K. to Assab and from there overland to the camps. The other method is by air to Addis Ababa and from there by road to the camps.

2 The severely malnourished need rehydration and non-solid food with a high energy content. The moderately malnourished need milk and biscuits to supplement home diets. The slightly malnourished need grain to bring the home diet up to the standard ration.

## Further questions

1 What is the critical height to weight ratio below which people are in immediate danger of death?
*70%*
2 What are the main kinds of food needed?
*Non-solids, milk, biscuits, grain.*
3 What is the standard grain ration per person?
*15 kilograms per month.*

## Target student commentary

The Oxfam weighing and measuring programme identifies the people at most risk, i.e. those with less than 70% normal weight to height ratio. These people need a 28 day constant care programme. Other categories need supplements to existing diets.

# Pages 38 and 39
# The Emergency Unit meets

Students are introduced to a meeting of the Emergency Unit, read background information on Ethiopia and then listen to part of the Emergency Unit meeting with the aim of completing information on the *Food, Health and nutrition* and *Shelter* sections of the grid. After this, roles could be allocated on the basis of the grid headings and students asked to make short presentations of the information found in the grids.

# The grid

## Language objective

1 Listening for and noting down missing numerical information.

### Note
The Oxfam Energy Biscuit was specially developed in the early 1980s for use as a supplementary food in disasters and emergencies. In cases of severe malnutrition, energy is the most important factor. The OEB therefore contains the maximum number of calories possible, while at the same time supplying sufficient protein.

## Target lexis

See pages 83 and 84 of the *Student's Book* for the tapescript.

## Answers to questions

### 1 Food
Grain *33 people/£115 per metric ton.*
Notes *Grain may kill the severely malnourished.*

### 2 Health and nutrition
Powdered milk *100 people/£588 per metric ton.*
Notes *Major part of diet/protein for body building.*
Oxfam Energy Biscuit *160 children/£1,300 per metric ton.*
Notes *Gives calories — not proteins/stopgap measure to keep people alive.*
Nurse-nutritionist *Number required = 1 per 1,000 patients.*
Cost *£9,000.*
Notes *Also need transport.*
Equipment: Land Rovers *Number required = 3. Cost = £10,000 each.*

### 3 Shelter
Blankets *£3.15 per unit.*
Notes *Shelter connected to food and energy!*
Plastic sheeting *£55 per roll.*
Notes *I roll covers 14 families, i.e. about 40 people.*

## Further questions

1 Why is grain unsuitable for the severely malnourished?
*Because digestion of it uses up vital reserves of energy.*
2 What is the function of the Oxfam Energy Biscuit?
*It is a stopgap measure to keep people alive until better food arrives.*
3 What is the connection between clothing and food?
*If people get cold, they use up energy that must be replaced.*
4 What is the approximate cost of boring permanent water holes at the three feeding centres assuming the use of hand pumps?
*£80-85,000. (Water team + pumps, piping and tanks.)*
5 What would be the transport cost of sending one ton of grain by air to Ethiopia?
*£780.*

## Target student commentary

It is clear from this meeting that one of the main factors to be decided is the question of urgency. Air transport costs are so high that this method of transport can only be used for emergency cases. It is therefore important to decide exactly how many people are at immediate risk. The exact mix of supplies for these people must then be decided. After this, the question of how to prevent the lower risk cases becoming emergency category cases must be dealt with. The balance between emergency action and medium- and long-term preventive action is at the centre of this situation.

# Page 40 **The latest news from Britain and Ethiopia**

Students learn that the total fund will be £4m and they also read a report containing the precise numbers and categories of people now in all the Oxfam feeding centres in this region. On the basis of this information and the previous grids, the students now have to start making their decisions about fund allocation.

## Oxfam field report

### Language objectives

1 Reading and reporting key elements of a document, e.g. *Tremaign says that the population of the centres is increasing at a rate of 10% per week.*
2 Summarizing a situation, e.g. *The feeding centre situation is grim and the only long-term hope is to solve the problem at village level.*
3 Estimating and presenting a numerical overview of a situation, e.g. *The emergency category now stand at 20,000 but will grow to 33,923 within one month.*

You should assume that the immediate needs relate directly to category 1, 70% w/h ratio, the short- to medium-term needs to category 2, 70-90% w/h ratio, and the long-term needs to category 3, 90% w/h ratio. It should become clear to the students that the key to the problem is to stop the mass migration from villages to feeding centres. This will mean persuading the 90% w/h category to stay in the villages by starting water projects and providing seed corn. The feeding centres would then become emergency centres for the worst cases.

As this part of the unit is an exercise in presenting and discussing figures, you may ask students to carry out the actual calculations individually and to present their calculations after, say, ten minutes. The

discussion could then revolve around a justification of the figures rather than item-by-item calculation.

## Answers to questions

**1 Items needed**
**a) immediate needs**
There are 20,000 people in the 70% w/h ratio and each of these will need a 28 day constant care programme based on i) powdered milk and ii) Oxfam Energy Biscuits. They will also need nurse/nutritionists to administer the programme.
**b) short- to medium-term needs**
There are 40,000 people in the 70-90% w/h category and each will need a supplementary feeding programme based on i) milk, ii) biscuit, iii) grain and iv) shelter.
**c) long-term needs**
There are 140,000 people. Each will need grain to bring them up to the standard family rations of 15 kilograms per person per month.

**2 Calculations**
**a) Immediate needs**
a) There are 20,000 people in this category. As 1 ton of powdered milk feeds 100 children for 60 days, it will feed 200 children for up to 30 days. They will therefore need 100 tons of milk at a cost of £58,800, ex-transport. Air transport costs = 100 x £780 = £78,000. Total milk costs = £136,000.
b) 1 ton of energy biscuits feeds 160 children for 60 days so 1 ton will feed about 320 children for 30 days. Thus they will need 62.5 tons at £1,300 per ton = £81,250. Air transport costs for 62.5 tons = £48,750. Total biscuit costs = £130,000. There will be additional overland transport costs for milk and biscuits of £19,500, i.e. 162.5 tons x £120.
c) Nurse/nutritionists at £9,000 each. 1:1,000 ratio = 20 at £9,000 = £180,000. With 3 Land Rovers = extra £30,000. Total = £210,000.
*Present emergency needs = £495,500*

But the 70% w/h category population is increasing at 10% per week. Within a month there will be a further 13,923 people in this category. This will mean further expenditure of £346,850. Total allocation for this category could be at around £842,350. To be on the safe side it might make sense to allocate £1m of the overall budget, i.e. 25%, to the emergency category.
*Total emergency needs over one month = £1,000,000.*

**b) Short- to medium-term needs**
Students will have to make various assumptions for this category, e.g. the combinations of milk, biscuit and grain will vary across the range of the 70-90% w/h ratios. Thus only a proportion of individuals in this category will need full milk and biscuit supplements. Say 50% will need full milk

supplement and 25% full energy biscuit supplement. Everyone will need grain at, say, 100% of standard family ration. Therefore:

**Powdered milk:** Take 60 days as the target feeding period. Thus 1 ton powdered milk feeds 100 people for 60 days. Assume a 50% supplement need. Thus 40,000 will need 50% of 400 tons = 200 tons. Cost = 200 x £588 = £117,600. Plus sea transport at £22 per ton = £4,400 and road transport at £120 per ton = £24,000. Total = £146,000.

**Energy biscuit:** 1 ton feeds 160 for 60 days. Assume 25% supplement need. Thus 40,000 will need 25% of 250 tons = 62.5 tons. Cost = £1,300 x 62.5 = £81,250. Assume half of this will go by air, the rest by sea. 31.25 tons x £780 = £24,375. 31.25 x £22 = £687. Overland transport = 62.5 x 120 = £7,500. Total = £113,812.

**Grain:** 1 ton feeds 33 people for 60 days. Therefore this category needs 1,212 tons at £115 per ton = £139,380. Sea transport at £22 per ton = £26,664. Road transport at £120 per ton = £145,440. Total cost = £311,484.

**Shelter:** 40,000 people will need the same number of blankets at £3.15 per unit = £126,000. Transport by sea of 20 tons = £440. Overland cost of 20 tons = £2,400. Sheeting could also be included here if students wish.
*Present short- to medium-term needs = £700,136.*

But this category is increasing (30% of the new arrivals, i.e. 30% of the overall 10% increase per week are in this category). Thus after one month there will be an extra 27,846 people in this category. Thus, approximately, a further £490,000 will be needed to cover the extra people.

Total cost of short- to medium-term needs over one month = £1,190,000. In other words, almost 30% of the £4m fund will be needed for this category.

### c) Long-term needs

This category is the key to everything. If they can solve the problem in the villages, then the migration to the camps can be stemmed and the problem of famine be halted at the village level. The first problem is to prevent the people in this category deteriorating further. This means massive grain shipments. The second problem is to build up the village infrastructures around new water supplies.

**Grain:** Assume a 75% supplement to bring the population up to the standard ration. 1 ton feeds 33 people for 60 days. Thus 140,000 people would need 4,242 tons x 75% = 3,181 tons. Cost = £365,815. Sea transport = £93,324. Road transport = £381,720. Total cost = £840,859.

**Shelter:** 140,000 blankets = £441,000. 3,500 rolls of plastic sheeting = £192,500. Sea transport costs = 140 tons x £22 = £3,080. Overland transport = 140 x £120 = £16,800.
*Present long-term needs = £1,494,239.*

But the weekly increase in this category is 55% of the new arrivals. This means that after one month there will be a further 51,051 people in this category. Thus the total extra cost would be £2,293,870.

Total long-term needs over one month = £3,788,109. In other words, the long-term needs of the expected feeding centre population after one month would use up almost all the £4m budget.

To stop the continuing move to the feeding centres, some of the £2.293m needed for future arrivals could be used to send emergency water teams to sink wells in the outlying villages.

**Water:** 10 towns - say 2 diesel pumps + 1,000 meters of piping each = 10 x £35,000 + £3,000 = £353,000. 200 villages - say one hand pump + 100 meters of piping each = £160,000. In addition, they would need, say, 10 water teams at £75,000 plus water tanks at £500 each = £750,000 + 210 x £500 = £105,000 = £855,000. Total water programme = £1,368,000.

### Summary

The £4m budget would adequately cover the situation in the feeding centres at present. Total present needs = £2,689,875. The problem is that the situation is deteriorating rapidly and in one month from now the total needs would amount to £5,978,109.

# Page 41 The Emergency Unit goes into action

The students will by now realize that the total cost of a full one month programme which covers food, health and shelter needs and a long-term water programme will be in excess of £6m. This is way beyond the forecast budget. Students therefore now have to decide what to leave out of their programme. To do this they will use the Ethiopia fund allocation grid in which exact allocations of funds and items may be made. At this point, students take roles within the Emergency Unit.

# Ethiopia fund allocation grid

## Language objectives

1 Arguing in a budget meeting for a particular course of action, e.g. *In my view, we have to find a balance between saving lives now and saving lives in the future.*
2 Presenting numerical estimates of different courses of action, e.g. *A full water programme will cost us £1.368m.*
3 Presenting counter-arguments, e.g. *But that will mean taking funds from immediate food needs.*
4 Negotiating and presenting compromise solutions to a problem, e.g. *Look, if we allocate £500,000 to a water programme, this will allow us to maintain a minimum feeding programme at the same time as making a start on the basic problem facing us.*

## Target lexis

| | | |
|---|---|---|
| to allocate | to forego | to terminate |
| allocation | to do without | to slash |
| fund | to decrease | to sacrifice |
| to reduce | to compromise | shortfall |
| to cut out | | |

## Answers to questions

2 **Emergency needs priorities**
To save as many lives as possible by transporting the necessary food, shelter and skills to the centres as quickly as possible. This category should have first claim on all funds.

**Short- and medium-term priorities**
To prevent serious cases in this category becoming emergency cases. To stabilize the majority of this category at their present w/h ratios through supplementary feeding. To encourage marginal individuals in this category to return to their villages with the promise of infrastructural improvements. To discourage further migration of this category to the centres through infrastructural improvements and perhaps by transporting grain to the villages.

**Long-term priorities**
To support present w/h ratios with supplementary rations. To encourage the whole of this category to return home through major infrastructure programmes, e.g. water programmes. To discourage further migration from the villages through a combination of water, seed corn, agricultural advisory services and local supplementary feeding programmes.

3 As shown above, a full programme including water and infrastructure would cost in excess of £6m which is £2m more than the forecast fund. Students should identify a shortfall of this approximate magnitude and then devise a way to spend the available fund most effectively. They should see that the major burden on resources is caused by the long-term categories who have not yet arrived, i.e. they will need extra resources valued at almost £2.3m which is almost the total shortfall. If ways can be found to keep these people working on the land, e.g. by taking water and agricultural advisory teams to the villages, then this huge burden will be slowly reduced. The decision which must be made, however, is how much to reduce these resources in order to improve their water and crop growing situation.

## Likely outcome

As about £2.2m of the available fund will be needed to provide for the emergency and short- and medium-term needs for one month, this leaves only about £1.8m available for the long-term needs. Over one month this would result in a shortfall of about £1.6m. This will only be the case if the people continue to flood into the feeding centres. Students may decide to start a village infrastructure programme including water teams, agricultural advisers and doctors to reduce the migration to the feeding centres. If they allocated £800,000 to this, they would then have £1m to spend on grain supplies for long-term needs. If people stay in their villages, the need for spending on shelter will be reduced. One possible final allocation may therefore be:

Emergency needs: £1m.
Short- and medium-term needs: £1.2m.
Long-term needs: Infrastructure programme: £0.8m.
Grain supplies: £1m.
Total: £4m.

**Note**
The final allocation of funds will vary from group to group. As long as students can justify their decisions and the expenditure is within budget, then, unlike in the real world, the case may be considered completed.

## Synopsis

A car component manufacturer faces complaints from its workers about procedures for mounting rubber seals. Although a tool has been provided, the workers have always used their hands to mount the seals as this is faster and improves their earnings on the company's piece rate system. Since the failure of their latest wage claim, the workers are complaining of a condition known as tenosinovitis (TSV). The workers' union takes up their case and threatens legal action. The company's lawyers refer to the relevant employment law and find that it is open to interpretation.

## Case objectives

1 Identifying and explaining differences between formal and informal working practices.
2 Analyzing and presenting the history of an industrial dispute.
3 Interpreting the legal aspects of an industrial dispute.
4 Devising a plan of action to deal with the dispute.

## Overall language objectives

1 Describing cause and effect in an employment dispute.
2 Using medical, legal and industrial relations terminology in a business situation.
3 Arguing a case for and against a particular work system.
4 Negotiating a settlement to an industrial dispute.

## Suggested preparation

Since this case revolves around aspects of employment law, a useful introduction to the case would be a review of key legal lexis, e.g. *law, contract, clause, case.* Ask students to study the legal extracts on page 45 before starting the unit.

## Classroom management

This unit adopts a case study approach until page 46 where students are required to take the roles of counsel for the employers, counsel for the employees and judge in the case. The unit could be completed as a case study with the students deciding as outsiders who has the best case.

## Page 42
# A severe case of TSV

Students read the introduction and study a definition from a medical dictionary. They learn that there has been a sudden increase in absence due to illness at Harmer Hydraulics and that sick notes indicate tenosinovitis as the cause of these absences.

## Tenosinovitis

### Answers to questions

2 It is caused by too much use of one or a group of muscles and a resulting build-up of oxidizing agents.
3 Complete rest of the muscle for twelve hours or longer rest for serious sufferers.

## Page 43 Background

Students read the background to the situation and discover that, although the workers had assembled the pistons manually for several years, they only began to complain after the failure of their wage negotiations. The students then listen to a conversation between Pamela Bridges and the union convenor and, finally, read a management memorandum concerning reaction on the shop floor.

### Background questions

1 What are the two methods for mounting the rubber parts onto the pistons?
   *Using a tool or manually.*
2 Why did the workers prefer the manual method?
   *Because they were on a piece rate system and could work faster with their hands.*
3 When did the workers first complain of sore hands?
   *When a supplier began to use stiffer rubber.*
4 When did the workers next complain about sore hands?
   *After the failure of the wage claim.*

## Target student commentary

It seems that the union convenor, Max Smith, is using a minor incident to score a negotiating point against management. Although the complaint is genuine in some cases, it would appear that an informal working agreement which evolved during times of prosperity has suddenly collapsed under the pressure of recession and the subsequent drop in worker morale.

## Conversation between Pamela Bridges and Max Smith

### Language objective

Listening to and reporting the gist of a conversation.

### Target lexis

| | |
|---|---|
| shift | bitterness |
| to have a chat about | shop floor |
| to stick to specifics | to hand things over to |
| to clear things up | hard line |
| to redesign | uncooperative |
| to suffer | uncompromising |
| injury | conciliatory |
| manual assembly | |

See page 84 of the *Student's Book* for the tapescript.

### Answers to questions

2 Smith is taking a hard line and is clearly in an uncompromising mood.
3 Bridges argues that the company would be prepared to modify the tools or change shift patterns. She also says that the company has been very reasonable in the past and that at first there were no complaints about the process.

### Further questions

1 How does Smith explain the absence of complaints in the first year?
  *He says it takes a long time for the medical condition to become obvious.*
2 Why is Smith no longer the key man?
  *Because he has handed the case over to his union's legal officer.*

### Target student commentary

It seems that Smith may be using the medical problem as an excuse for bringing up the pay issue again. It is unclear, however, whether he sees the medical problem as a bargaining lever to make the company reconsider the pay claim or as a kind of revenge for his lack of success at the negotiations.

## Harmer Hydraulics memorandum

### Language objective

Scanning a text for specific information.

### Target lexis

| | | |
|---|---|---|
| to stir things up | swollen | warning signs |
| impression | to claim | benefit of the doubt |
| to monitor | aches and pains | to diagnose |
| discomfort | genuine | discontent |
| locker room | to admit | |

### Answers to questions

2 There is obviously discontent on the shop floor but this is probably being encouraged and made worse by Smith.
3 A few people are suffering from genuine TSV but the others so far have only slight aches and pains. The doctor, however, has to give everyone the benefit of the doubt.

### Further questions

1 According to Jack Hubbard, when do the pains begin?
  *When the workers have stopped working.*
2 What real evidence is there of a medical problem?
  *One man had swollen hands and two or three others were in genuine pain.*
3 How is Max Smith dealing with the situation?
  *He is telling everyone with an ache or pain that it could be a warning of something more serious.*

### Target student commentary

There is obviously a real problem on the shop floor and Max Smith may be very worried about the health of his members. The company clearly believes that he is using the situation for his own purposes.

---

# Page 44
# A letter from the union

---

Students read a letter in which the union makes certain demands and indicates that it has a good case in law against the company.

## The United Motor Workers' Union letter

### Language objectives

1 Reading a letter for its gist.
2 Reading a letter for specific information.
3 Identifying the register and style of official letters.

## Target lexis

| | |
|---|---|
| to inform | to contravene |
| intentions | to find in favour of |
| with respect to | to proceed with the matter |
| incidence of | to settle the matter out of court |
| irrefutable | lump sum |
| working practices | notification |

### Note

A consolidated wage rate is a payment system in which previously separate elements of earnings are combined in one wage, e.g. a payment based on results may now become part of the standard wage which is not based on direct results.

## Answers to questions

1 The gist of the letter is that the union is threatening to take legal action unless the company agrees to certain things.
2 It thinks it can win the case on the basis of the Health and Safety at Work Act. But it will not go to court if the company agrees to its proposals.
3 To modify the tool; to get rid of the piece rate system and replace it with higher wages; to provide £3,000 compensation for each injured worker.

## Further questions

1 What evidence does the union have against Harmer Hydraulics?
*30 notifications of illness accompanied by medical certificates.*
2 What basis does it want for the consolidated wage rate?
*The last quarter's average earnings under the piece rate system.*

## Target student commentary

The union is taking a hard line but seems to be interested mainly in reopening the negotiations about wages. It is threatening to use the Health and Safety at Work Act against the company but this is possibly only a ploy to gain concessions from Harmer.

---

# Page 45 **A question of law**

---

Students read about a past legal battle between Harmer and the union and then study the precise wording of the relevant clauses in the Health and Safety at Work Act.

## The Health and Safety at Work Act

### Language objective

Studying a legal text and interpreting it in your own words.

### Target lexis

| | |
|---|---|
| duty | preceding |
| substance | to ensure |
| provision | supervision |
| reasonably practicable | absence of |
| omissions | welfare |
| handling | to impose on |
| without prejudice to | storage |
| statutory provision | generality |
| article | to comply with |

### Answers to questions

2 **2 (1)** Every employer must make sure his or her workers are not in danger in the workplace.
  **2 (2)** Specific responsibilities of the employer are:
    a) safe equipment and working systems.
    b) safe handling, storage and transportation systems.
    c) sufficient training and supervision to avoid danger to employees.
  **6 (1)** Designers and makers of tools and equipment must:
    a) make sure they are safe when used properly.
  **7** Every employee must:
    a) make sure their own acts do not endanger themselves or others.
    b) cooperate with the employer to observe the safety rules.

3 The union can argue:
  **2 (1)** the company did not make sure there was no danger in the workplace, i.e. the piece rate system encouraged avoidance of tools and systems.
  **2 (2)** a - the company's piece rate system was part of the system of work and contributed to lack of safety.
  **2 (2)** b and c - the arrangements for handling were not risk-free and were not enforced through supervision.
  **7 a** - the workers took reasonable care of their health but were not informed of the dangers of manual assembly by the company.
  **7 b** - the workers cooperated with management at all stages.

**4** The company can argue:

**2 (1)** it did everything practicable to ensure safety, e.g. it went back to softer rubber when the problem started.

**2 (2) a** - it provided completely safe tools.

**2 (2) b** - it provided safe handling systems.

**2 (2) c** - it trained and supervised workers as much as was practicable.

**6 (1)** - the tools were of a safe design.

**7 (a)** - the workers did not take care of their own health because they refused to use the tools.

## Target student commentary

Clearly, Harmer could argue that he has provided all the necessary equipment and training to ensure safety. He could also cite Section 7b to show that the workforce did not cooperate to allow him to carry out his duties fully. The union could argue that the company forced an unpopular piece rate system on them and paid only lip service to the legal requirements. Also, it did not provide proper supervision to ensure the use of the equipment.

---

# Page 46 Decision

---

Students hold a meeting to discuss the legal position for both sides in the upcoming court case, using the *agenda for meeting to be held to discuss TSV problem*. They do this as outsiders. (As an alternative, roles could be assigned at this point so that the students can, in small groups or individually, use the agenda to prepare their case before going into court.)

They then take on the roles of legal counsel for the company, legal counsel for the union and judge in the case. (The simulation could be negotiations towards an out-of-court-settlement.)

## Decision/Agenda for meeting

### Language objective

Taking part in an informal meeting to discuss a situation with a view to devising a plan of action.

### Answers to questions

**2 Harmer Hydraulics' main arguments**

a) The company has a good health and safety record, provides its own medical staff and received very few complaints until the breakdown of pay negotiations.

b) The company has provided and maintained plant and equipment to ensure the safety and health of its workers.

c) The company provided a safe tool.

d) The company trained and supervised the workers to use the tool.

e) The workers refused to cooperate in the use of the tool and preferred to work with their hands.

f) There were no complaints until the union convenor failed to win a wage claim. He is now undertaking a personal vendetta against the company.

**3 The United Motor Workers' Union main arguments**

a) The company has had judgements made against them in the past in the area of employee safety, e.g. the chip incident.

b) The workers complained about the use of the tool a year previously but nothing was done.

c) The company made it impossible to achieve satisfactory earnings using the tool and therefore put pressure on the workforce to use their hands.

d) The tool is inadequate for the job when used in the present piece rate system.

e) The company tacitly accepted the manual method and therefore failed to ensure the safety and health of its employees.

f) The present incidence of TSV has been confirmed by medical staff at the company.

## The courtroom proceedings

### Language objectives

1 Putting forward arguments and counter-arguments according to a given position.

2 Persuading and dissuading.

3 Summing up an argument.

**Note**

Students are obviously not expected to adopt a legalistic turn-of-phrase during the simulation but the tone of the verbal interactions should be fairly formal, given that the students are taking the parts of lawyers and the judge or judges in the case.

### Harmer's bargaining points

a) Compensation only for injury which can be proved by rigorous medical tests.

b) Modification of the tool to speed up production.

c) Replacement of the present manual/semi-manual systems by automated systems which will mean job losses.

d) Scrapping of piece-rate system and replacement by bonus system based on results.

e) Willingness to take the case to court if no agreement can be reached out of court.

**Union's bargaining points**
a) The confirmed and suspected cases of TSV among the workforce must be compensated.
b) Adverse publicity if the matter reaches the press.
c) Willingness to accept improved wage levels or modification of piece rate system.
d) Willingness to take some form of industrial action, e.g. work-to-rule, strike.
e) Willingness to argue the case in court.

## Likely outcome

Although it was the workers who originally adopted manual assembly techniques rather than use the tools provided, the company acquiesced in these practices because they led to higher productivity. It could be argued, therefore, that the company did not comply with Section 2(c) of the Act. On the other hand, it could be argued that the workers did not comply with Section 7(b) when they failed to use the tools provided, even when reminded of their existence after the problem of the stiff rubber. The company could argue that the union is trying to use the law to promote a straightforward industrial dispute about wages. The union could say that the company failed to provide adequate tools to maintain the levels of productivity required and thus failed to comply with Article 2 Section 1. There is nothing in the Act, however, that links safety with productivity levels. For this reason, the employer is likely, although not necessarily, to win the case on points.

# The oil rig

## Synopsis

This is a group activity which will test the students' ability to work together. It involves the construction of a model oil rig structure using only four milk or wine bottles and three standard table knives which you will need to supply.

## Suggested exploitation

1 Ask students to read through the introduction and report on the history of and present situation in Vitrasia.
2 Ask students to describe the tender document and establish the final targets for the activity, i.e. *an oil rig which will support a milk bottle full of water even when a student blows at full force at the bottle.*
3 Suggest useful language items for the activity, e.g. *Why don't we...? I think we should... I suggest... No, not like that!*
4 Divide students into pairs or small groups and issue them with the necessary materials. Give them a time limit with which to come up with a model. A reasonable period would be fifteen minutes. The solution to the problem is as follows. You may need to give tips if students find it hard going.

5 Ask students to present their models using the appropriate presentation language.
6 Test each model with the full blow test and be prepared for accidents! Award the contract to the best solution.

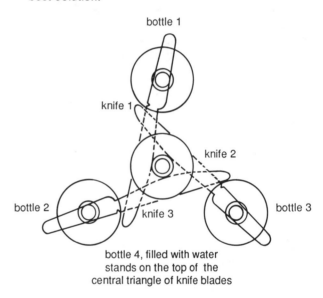

bottle 4, filled with water stands on the top of the central triangle of knife blades

# Unit 10 Autotech and the electronic map

## Synopsis
This case is about a highly specialized car component manufacturer which has a technical success on its hands but lacks the means or size to exploit it. Students have to devise the best strategy to bring a top-of-the-market, specialist product to a wider volume market. The problem is complicated by a mass market competitor which suddenly announces its own version of the product and threatens to take over the market completely.

**Note**
This case is extended in *Unit 11 Please, Mr Banker?* for those students interested in the financial aspects of the case. In Unit 11 Autotech's profit and loss accounts and balance sheets are studied in order to plan a financial strategy for expansion.

## Case objectives
1 Identifying and discussing the arguments for and against remaining a producer of expensive, specialist products in a market which seems to be moving towards volume production.
2 Identifying the implications of major expansion for any manufacturing company.
3 Analyzing various methods of achieving rapid expansion of production and marketing activities.
4 To devise the best strategy for a small company to maintain its hi-tech market leader position in the face of a major competitive attack in a rapidly expanding market.

## Overall language objectives
1 Identifying and presenting the main features and benefits of a product.
2 Arguing for and against a particular competitive strategy.
3 Analyzing, presenting and discussing the structure of an industry in terms of suppliers and producers.

## Suggested preparation
Pages 48 and 49 provide the introductory information to this unit. This information, which consists of an advertisement, a factory capacity chart and an internal memo, could be studied by students as preparatory homework and presented by them in class.

## Classroom management
This unit adopts a case study approach until page 52 where students take part in an Autotech meeting to decide a plan of action.

## Page 48 Autotech and the electronic map

Students read the background to the case and study an advertisement.

## Announcing the Autotech Automap Mk 2

### Language objectives
1 Presenting the features of a technical product, e.g. *The Automap Mk 2 features an LCD screen and a keyboard for accessing information.*
2 Presenting the benefits of a technical product, e.g. *The two major benefits of the Automap are shorter journey times and reduced fuel consumption.*
3 Identifying and explaining the strategy behind an advertisement, e.g. *It is targetted at motor manufacturers and stresses the unique selling point that such a map would give to their cars.*

### Target lexis
| | | |
|---|---|---|
| invention | advantage | hold-up |
| innovation | to display | availability |
| trade press | radius | keyboard |
| benefit | to calculate | |

**Note**
LCD = liquid crystal display
Best 'call' sequence = the best route and sequence of sales visits

### Answers to questions
2 The main features are an LCD screen containing the map and a section for digital information, a keyboard and map disc drives.
3 It shows the area within a 150 kilometre radius of the car.
It shows the exact present position of the car on the map.
It calculates and shows the shortest route.
It calculates the best fuel efficiency speeds.
It lists and locates road services, e.g. hotels.
It shows hold-ups ahead.
It calculates the best 'call' sequences for salesmen.

### Further questions
1 Who is the advertisement aimed at?
*Car manufacturers.*
2 What will the basic list price per unit be?
*Under £500.*

## Target student commentary

The Automap Mk 2 is the latest version of the original Automap but is designed to reach a wider market. The main features of this revolutionary product are a screen which displays a moving map, a keyboard on which a driver can request information and map disc drives. The main advantages of the Automap are instant information about the car's position and movement, the ability to discover the shortest route to a destination and to check services and problems for miles ahead. The overall benefit will be a reduction in motoring costs.

---

# Page 49 **Small is beautiful**

---

Students read about John Lyle's background, study and discuss his company's present production capacity, and then read a memo summing up the present Automap Mk 2 marketing strategy.

## Autotech factory capacity and output bar chart

### Language objectives

1 Analyzing and describing bar chart information, e.g. *This shows that capacity has been expanding steadily.*
2 Describing and discussing production figures, e.g. *Output rose from 15,000 units in 1990 to 40,000 units in 1992.*
3 Describing and discussing factory capacity utilization, e.g. *Capacity expansion has always been kept slightly ahead of production needs.*

### Target lexis

| | | |
|---|---|---|
| to utilize | to expand | to match |
| excess capacity | output | demand |
| under capacity | constraints | to keep up with |

### Answers to questions

2 Each year Lyle has expanded capacity to meet the following year's demand.
3 The Mk 2 will be launched at the end of 1992 and factory capacity has been more than doubled to allow production of 40,000 units of the Mk 2 in 1993.

## Target student commentary

In the last three years Autotech has, on average, doubled its capacity each year. Although production of the Mk 1 is expected to start levelling off in 1993, the company expects to sell 40,000 units of the Mk 2 in its first year of production. Its total anticipated production of both Automap versions in 1993 is 90,000 units.

## Automap Mk 2: Sales programme

### Language objective

Identifying and summarizing the core of a strategy, e.g. *They will target the fleet car market through manufacturers and through fleet companies, and establish the product as a technical success before promoting it more vigorously.*

### Answers to questions

2 Fleet car manufacturers and purchasers.
3 He will only expand production when demand justifies it. He will ask manufacturers to install the Automap as an optional extra rather than a standard feature. He wants to prove the quality of the product technically first.

---

# Page 50 **... but big is sometimes necessary**

---

Students read a specialist magazine article which will change the whole situation for John Lyle and force him to take major decisions about his company's future.

## Autotronics puts itself on the electronic map

### Language objectives

1 Reading for specific information, e.g. *The competitive product will sell for about £290.*
2 Predicting the implications of new information upon an existing situation, e.g. *This news will mean that Autotech must either expand fast or sell its product as licences.*

### Answers to questions

2 a) Autotronics is Britain's largest autocomponents manufacturer.
b) The Navitron 1 is Autotronics' version of the electronic map. It will sell for about £290 and is aimed at the fleet car market.

3 The implications are serious because Autotronics has the power to dominate the market in terms of production and price.

## Further questions

1 What savings can the motorist expect from the electronic map?
*A 15% cut in motoring costs.*
2 What is the rumour in the market?
*That Autotronics is about to sign a contract with a major motor manufacturer.*

## Target student commentary

The news of the Navitron 1 changes the situation completely. If Autotronics signs a deal with one of the big three motor manufacturers, it could mean that Autotech will be squeezed out of the market. John Lyle must now make a decision. Should he expand fast and try to win a similar contract for the Mk 2 or should he stay small, produce only the Mk 1 for the top end of the market and sell the Mk 2 as a licence?

# Page 51
# Autotech: which way now?

Students read about how John Lyle faces up to the crisis, study the supply structure of the motor industry and calculate the period it would take for a buyer of the Automap Mk 2 to recoup their expenditure through reduced motoring costs.

## European fleet car manufacturers and their electrical and electronic component suppliers

### Language objectives

1 Describing the structure of an industry, e.g. *The European fleet car industry breaks down into three major producers and three smaller manufacturers.*
2 Describing the supply structure of an industry, e.g. *Although the fleet car manufacturers produce 30% of their own components, four independent component manufacturers supply a further 65%.*
3 Identifying and expressing opportunities and threats, e.g. *One possibility would be to offer the Automap to one of the smaller fleet manufacturers.*

### Target lexis

| | | |
|---|---|---|
| pie chart | to break down | proportion |
| supplier | to be dominated by | to purchase |
| parts | share | to source |
| | segment | |

## Answers to questions

2 The dominant manufacturers are European Motors with 35% of the market, Global Motors with 28% and Scanmotors with 22%. The dominant suppliers are the manufacturers themselves (30% of the market) and Autotronics (25%).
3 Autotech is not even mentioned among the smaller suppliers on this chart and so it must be assumed that it is in the 'others' section. It is clearly far too small at present to become a supplier of volume components to the manufacturers. It must decide whether it can expand capacity on its own or link up with one of the larger suppliers or even approach one of the manufacturers with a view to setting up a joint venture. Alternatively, it could sell licences either to a supplier or a manufacturer.

## Further questions

1 How many fleet cars are sold in Europe each year?
*2m.*
2 If European Motors installed the Automap in all its fleet cars, how many units would be needed?
*700,000, i.e. 35% x 2m units.*
3 What would be the total value of the deal if the unit price was £400?
*£280m*

## Target student commentary

The fleet car market is dominated by three major manufacturers. At the same time, component suppliers are few and the largest one is Autotronics with 25% of the market. If Autotronics has done a deal with European Motors then it may be in Autotech's interest to approach Scanmotors or Global Motors, both of whom will be interested in protecting their positions in the market with this new car accessory. The major problem is still how to finance the huge production runs necessary to supply a major car manufacturer. Autotech could approach the fleet users direct and persuade them to adopt the Automap by demonstrating its cost-saving potential.

## I.R.R.I. cost-benefit study

### Language objectives

1 Describing the payback period on a customer's expenditure, e.g. *The payback period on the Automap would be less than two years for the average user.*
2 Justifying a purchasing decision on the basis of performance figures, e.g. *The Automap would reduce fuel consumption by about 4% per year.*

## Answers to questions

2  £302, i.e. Present annual fuel bills = £1,897
(40,225 ÷ 10.6 x £0.5).
6% kilometre reduction and 4% lower fuel
consumption result in annual fuel bill of £1,715
(40,225 − 2,413 = 37,812).
10.16 ltrs per km + 0.424 = 11.024 (37,812 ÷
11.024 x £0.5 = £1,715).
Deduct also residual saving of £10 per month, i.e.
£120 = £1,595. Thus total annual saving = £302.

3  1.62 years, i.e. total cost of Automap = £490 ÷
£302 = 1.62 years.

## Further question

1  What will be the net benefit to the Automap user
over the average life of a fleet car?
*£265, i.e. Annual savings of £302 x 2.5 = £755.*
*Deduct cost of Automap at £490 = £265.*

## Target student commentary

Autotech will clearly be able to demonstrate tangible
cost savings to users of the Automap Mk 2. Over the
average life of a fleet car, Automap will provide a total
saving of about £755. With a price per unit of £490,
this will mean that Automap will pay for itself in just
over 18 months and give a net benefit over 2.5 years
of about £265. There will also be various intangible
benefits. Initial curiosity and status value will bring
extra advantages to fleet owners, e.g. more rental
customers to car hire companies and also a reduction
in depreciation rates.

---

# Page 52  Action!

---

Students now divide into specialist groups and hold a
meeting using the agenda presented in the memo.
Their aim is to decide the future of Autotech. Students
should review, if necessary, the language of meetings
provided on page ix of the *Student's Book*.

## Internal memo

### Language objectives

See pages vii and ix of the *Language reference unit*.

## Likely outcome

The main options open to the company are as follows:

1  Go it alone with an expansion into the high volume
market, i.e. raise funds from outside sources in order
to expand the business by a factor of 5 or 6.
**For:** The potential market offers a major opportunity
for successful expansion.
**Against:** The risks are high and the company may
either have to take on large debts or to accept new
share participation which may reduce Lyle's control of
his company. Methods for raising funds include bank
loans, floating the company on the stock exchange, or
selling shares privately.

2  Reject expansion and consolidate its activities
around the present low volume – high value approach
with an emphasis on staying ahead technologically.
**For:** They are leaders in this sector and the risks are
low.
**Against:** The company will never be in a position to
exploit the rapidly expanding market for its own
inventions and may always be vulnerable to the large
scale manufacturers.

3  Sell the licences for the new product to other
manufacturers and receive income from royalties.
**For:** Further investment and risk will be minimized.
**Against:** Know-how will be sold to the market and
Autotech may be reduced to an R&D group with no
manufacturing activity.

4  Enter into a collaborative venture either with
another components producer or with one of the car
manufacturers.
**For:** Risk and investment will be shared.
**Against:** There will be some loss of control.

5  Sell Autotech and the inventions at a very high
price to the highest bidder to allow John Lyle to retire
comfortably.
The outcome will depend on the arguments put
forward by students. Most companies with major new
inventions would find it difficult to resist expansion
and, therefore, the most likely outcome would be
either a collaborative deal with one of the other
component manufacturers or a share flotation with a
view to financing expansion through the stock
markets.

**Note:**
If you do not wish to use the simulation approach at
the end of the unit you can continue the case
approach by holding a round table discussion to
examine the options open to Autotech. You can lead
students through the problem using the agenda on 52.

# Pause for thought 5

## The bottle experiment

### Synopsis
This *Pause for thought* provides the basis for a discussion of how purely logical thinking may hinder creativity. The purely rational and highly structured approach to problem-solving and new product development in companies may not always be the best or most efficient way of staying ahead of the competition. The flies in the experiment suggest that haphazard and random experimentation tends to free companies from fossilized ways of thinking. Companies that spend huge amounts of money on strictly controlled research and development departments may find that encouraging a climate of trial and error and random innovation may pay dividends.

### Suggested exploitation
1 Ask students to read the passage and then to describe the experiment in their own words.
2 Ask students to interpret the results of the bottle experiment. Elicit interpretations, if necessary, by asking questions, e.g. *Why did the wasps fail to find the exit? Why did the flies succeed?*
3 Write the following words and phrases on the whiteboard or OHP and ask students to guess or explain their meaning: *tunnel vision, mind set, lateral thinking, creative thinking, convergent thinking, divergent thinking, fossilization, brainstorming.*
4 Ask students to identify the words which point to the problem of fixed thought patterns, i.e. *tunnel vision, mind set, fossilization,* and then ask students to identify the words that point to methods of overcoming these phenomena. Ask students to explain how these help to overcome the problem of fixed thinking.
5 Then start a group discussion to interpret the implications, if any, for a company and its development and planning processes. To help this discussion on its way, you may like to ask individual students to describe their own company's approach to research and development and any problems which may have arisen.

# Unit 11 Please, Mr Banker?

## Synopsis

This is a specialized unit designed for students who are interested in finance, banking, accountancy and senior management strategy. Although it may be used on its own, it derives its storyline from *Unit 10 Autotech and the electronic map.* In Unit 10, John Lyle, Chairman of Autotech has to decide whether to remain a small specialist manufacturer or expand into volume production. In this unit, Lyle approaches a merchant bank to discuss ways of raising new capital for expansion.

## Case objectives

1 Analyzing a company's performance and overall financial condition on the basis of its Profit and Loss Statements Summaries and Balance Sheet over three years.
2 Devising and presenting a business plan with a view to raising capital for expansion.
3 Choosing the best way to raise the finance necessary for major expansion.

## Overall language objectives

1 Using the language of profit and loss accounts and balance sheets.
2 Presenting financial statements and answering questions about them.
3 Asking questions about financial statements and company performance.
4 Presenting a business plan for potential investors based on a company's past performance, present condition and future plans.

## Suggested preparation

You will need to check that the students fully understand the terminology of the financial documents on pages 55 and 56. Definitions of the terms used are given on pages 52-54 of this book.

Once this has been done, students analyze the numerical elements of the financial statements on pages 55-56 for homework. This will allow them time to make the necessary calculations ahead of the case study and simulation.

Students who have not yet done Unit 10 should study that unit for homework to get the background.

## Classroom management

This unit adopts a case study approach until page 57 where students take part in a meeting between Autotech and the Hunter-Benson Bank to devise a financial strategy for the company.

## Page 54 Please, Mr Banker?

Students listen to a telephone call between John Lyle, Chairman of Autotech and Mark Hampshire of the Hunter-Benson Bank, and then read a letter setting out Autotech's financial requirements.

## Telephone conversation between Lyle and Hampshire

### Language objective

Listening for specific information.

### Target lexis

| | |
|---|---|
| associate | expansion |
| profit and loss account | to handle |
| mainstream | cash flow forecast |
| share flotation | balance sheet |
| to read between the lines | |

See pages 84-85 of the Student's Book for the tapescript.

### Answers to questions

2 He requires finance to expand Autotech.
3 He needs information on Autotech including its plans and requirements, its balance sheets and profit and loss statements for the last three years, and a presentation of the new product.

### Target student commentary

Lyle has clearly decided to expand his business and now needs to arrange the finance for this expansion. Hampshire wants to make an assessment of the company's credit rating by looking at its financial statements for the last three years and the new product.

## Autotech letter to Hunter-Benson

### Language objective

Reading for specific information, e.g. *Autotech is planning to expand capacity to 400,000 units per year.*

### Answers to questions

2 He needs a total capital injection of £18m. £2m of this would be for R&D, £500,000 for sales and the rest for factory and production expansion.

# Pages 55-56 The banker and the industrialist

Students study Autotech's Profit and Loss Statements and Balance Sheet Summaries for the last three years. They then do some calculations and begin to build up a picture of the company's recent performance and overall financial health. Students will need pocket calculators for this activity.

## Autotech Profit and Loss Statements

### Language objectives

1 Analyzing and presenting the revenue, cost and profitability relationships over the period of the statements, e.g. *Pre-tax profits increased more quickly than turnover during this period.*
2 Summarizing a company's performance, e.g. *Autotech's P&L statements show that the company expanded rapidly over the three years and showed a healthy rise in profitability.*

### Answers to questions at the top of the page

1 If Autotech won a contract with, say, Scanmotors, it could sell up to 440,000 units of the Mk 2 in one year. (See page 51 of the *Student's Book* for the diagram.) At a price of £490 per unit this would generate revenues in the region of £216m.
2 See the definitions below.
3 See the definitions on pages 53-54.

### Profit and Loss Statement terminology

**Profit and Loss Statement**
Sometimes called a *Revenue account* in the U.K. and an *Income Statement* in the U.S.A., this statement is often described as a company's annual *scorecard*. In other words, it shows how well the company did in terms of profit and loss and how that *score* came about. It shows three major aspects of the profit/loss situation:
1 How the profit/loss was earned.
2 How much was taken in taxation.
3 How the after-tax profit/loss was used.

**Turnover** The total value of sales less VAT and discounts in any one period of time.
**Cost of sales** This does not relate to the sale of goods but to their production, i.e. the cost of producing the goods which are eventually sold. It will include all the costs of production such as factory wages, materials and production overheads such as depreciation of plant and equipment.

**Gross profit** This is the difference between the final selling price of the goods and the cost of producing the goods but before the company has deducted the non-manufacturing overhead costs involved in selling, distribution and administration.
**Distribution costs** All costs involved in getting the products to the customer, e.g. transport, insurance.
**Administration costs** All costs involved in running the overall administration of a company, e.g. salaries, buildings.
**R & D** (Research and Development) All costs involved in this activity.
**Depreciation of non-manufacturing assets** Depreciation means the spreading the initial costs of machinery and buildings over the years of their use. In this case, it refers to the cost of administration buildings, typewriters, cars, etc. Depreciation of plant and machinery appears in **Cost of sales** above.
**Interest payable** This is the interest the company must pay to lenders, e.g. banks, and relates to the **Long-term loans** item in the Balance Sheet.

**Net profit before tax** ( Pre-tax profit) Gross profit less the non-production overheads involved in running a company.
**Corporation tax** The tax that all companies have to pay on profit, i.e. the business equivalent of income tax.

**Net profit after tax** Net profit before tax less Corporation tax.

**Retained profit b/f** (brought forward) This is profit from the previous year which was not distributed to shareholders but which was kept within the company to finance production and expansion, for example, and is now brought forward to this year's accounts.

**Dividends payable** The part of profit which is distributed to shareholders.

**Retained profits c/f** (carried forward) The profit that will be kept within the company for purposes of finance and production expansion. This amount will be carried forward to the next period's P&L account since it will be used in that period. (Sometimes referred to as *ploughed back profit.*)

### Answers to questions at the bottom of the page

2 a) Turnover rose over the three years by 191% from £8.25m in 1990 to £24m in 1992.
   b) The ratio of labour to turnover has fallen from 26% in 1990 to 16.6% in 1992 indicating a considerable improvement in productivity.
   c) R&D expenditure has grown in real terms from £0.976m in 1990 to £2.374m in 1992 but has fallen as a % of turnover from 11.8% in 1990 to 9.9% in 1992.

d) Profit before tax as a proportion of turnover rose from 1.5% in 1990 to 15.6% in 1992.

e) Interest payments rose from £48,000 in 1990 to £579,000 in 1992.

f) Payment of dividends increased from £20,000 to £500,000 over the period.

3 The Profit and Loss Statements over the three years show that the company has expanded rapidly over this period. Production costs, on the whole, rose less than turnover and the pre-tax profit figures show a healthy increase in relation to sales. As would be expected in such an expansion, general non-manufacturing overheads rose substantially although special effort has clearly been put into R&D. The increase in interest payable shows that part of the expansion has been financed by increased bank loans. The only worry is that the cost of materials rose substantially more than either turnover or labour costs over the period and, if this trend continues, it may cause problems later. Overall, the Statements seem to indicate a balanced and well-controlled expansion.

# Balance Sheet Summaries

## Language objectives

1 Analyzing and expressing the significant relationships within a balance sheet, e.g. *The company's liquidity seems satisfactory although its collection period has increased.*

2 Summarizing the overall financial picture, e.g. *The company has a strong balance sheet in terms of its present activity levels.*

## Balance Sheet terminology

**Balance Sheet** This is not a scorecard like the Profit and Loss Statement but a sort of map showing how a company's finances are arranged at a particular moment in time, i.e. the date of the statement. It shows two main things:

a) Where the total amount of money represented by a company comes from, i.e. who owns it.

b) Where the total amount of money in a company goes to, i.e. how it is used.

The items which show how a company's money is used or tied up are called *assets* and the items which show who owns the money tied up in the assets are called *liabilities*, i.e. what the company as a legal entity would have to pay to particular individuals or institutions if the company were wound up. It should be noted that in British Balance Sheets, the *liabilities* used to appear on the left and the *assets* on the right. Today, the vertical format shown here is often preferred since it relates assets to liabilities in a way which allows quicker analysis of the company's overall position.

**Fixed Assets** These are long-term tangible assets such as machinery, buildings and plant and long-term intangible assets such as goodwill.

**Net written down value** This means that the original values of the items are shown in the Balance Sheet less the amounts of that original value that have been written off (depreciated) in previous years.

**Current assets** These are short-term assets usually related directly to present production, e.g. stocks of finished goods, goods still in production (work in progress) and cash. Current assets should usually be financed by short-term liabilities.

**Stock and work in progress** is usually items used for production but still in the state in which they were purchased.

**Work in progress** is goods in half-finished condition or finished goods. These items are sometimes referred to as *inventories* or *stocks*.

**Debtors** These represent amounts owing to the company, e.g. from customers who have not yet paid for their purchases. These are often called *Trade debtors*. Debtors are called *Receivables* in U.S. balance sheets.

**Cash in bank** This is money held in current or short-term company bank accounts.

**Current liabilities** These are short-term liabilities.

**Creditors** These are amounts owed by the company to suppliers in the short term.

**Accruals** This is an item of future liability due to work, supplies or a service which have been only partly received. An example of this would be rent that has to be paid annually in arrears on the 31st December. If the company's accounting period ends on November 30th, it has not yet had to pay the amount although it has received the benefit of its tenancy for 11/12ths of its annual value. If the rent is £1,000 for example, its accrued value would be £916.6 (11/12ths of £1,000).

**Taxation** This is Corporation tax due to the government. It does not include VAT.

**Capital employed** This is sometimes called *Net assets* and consists of the amount of money owned by shareholders and major lenders in the company. It consists of total assets less current liabilities. It is this amount against which profits may be compared to give a good measure of the company's performance, i.e. Return on capital employed.

**Share capital** Ownership of the company is divided into monetary units called shares, in this case 8m £1 shares. Shares are sometimes referred to as *equity*.

**Share premium** When new shares are issued above the par value of the existing shares, the nominal value of the shares is added to the issued share value and the difference between the new price and the par value, i.e. the premium value, is recorded in a separate share premium account.

**Retained profits** Profits kept in the company and not distributed to shareholders as dividends.

**Shareholders' funds** This is the total amount of capital owned by shareholders as distinct from lenders and consists of share capital, share premiums, retained profits and reserves.

**Long-term loans** Long-term bank loans to the company with fixed rates of interest and repayment dates.

## Notes on the ratio analysis of balance sheets

There are various standard ratio measures which are simple enough to calculate and can be fun to use in simulations. They allow students to make an initial assessment of a company's performance and situation. The subject is a large and complex one but for the purposes of a simulation or case study the following ratios should suffice:

a) **The liquidity ratio** = $\dfrac{\text{Liquid assets (debtors} \pm \text{cash)}}{\text{Current liabilities}}$

This shows whether a company can meet its short-term obligations from its liquid assets, e.g. cash. Rule of thumb is 1:1 and below that could mean company is having liquidity problems.
Autotech's liquidity ratio = 1990 - 1.2:1 (900/740.4)
    1991 - .96:1 (1800/1873)
    1992 - 1.05:1 (4400/4180)

b) **The current ratio** = $\dfrac{\text{Current assets}}{\text{Current liabilities}}$

This shows the cushion that short-term creditors could have against shortfalls in realizable value of current assets. Rule of thumb is 2:1.
Autotech's current ratio = 1990 - 2.14:1(587/740)
    1991 - 1.62:1(3050/1873)
    1992 - 1.60:1(6700/4180)

c) **Return on capital employed** = $\dfrac{\text{Net profit}}{\text{Capital employed}}$

This is the main profitability ratio and allows bankers to compare a company's performance with similar companies in the industry.
Autotech's return on capital employed = 1990 - 2.39%
    1991 - 22.4%
    1992 - 23.6%

d) **Profit on sales** = $\dfrac{\text{Net profit}}{\text{Turnover}}$

This shows the overall profit margins achieved on sales. Autotech's profit on sales = 1990 - 1.52%
    1991 - 14.75%
    1992 - 15.56%

e) **Debtors ratio** (Collection Period)

= $\dfrac{\text{Debtors}}{\text{Sales}}$ x 365 = x days.

This shows the effectiveness of credit control procedures and allows comparison with payment periods to creditors.
Autotech's collection period =
    1990 - 31 days (700/8250 x 365)
    1991 - 31.6 days(1300/15000 x 365)
    1992 - 45.6 days(3000/24000 x 365)

f) **Creditors ratio** (Payment period)

= $\dfrac{\text{Creditors}}{\text{Purchases}}$ (calculated, say, at 60% of turnover) x 365 = y days.

This shows how much the business is financed by trade creditors and allows comparison with collection period above.
Autotech's payments period =
    1990 - 44.2 days (600/4950 x 365)
    1991 - 40.5 days(1000/9000 x 365)
    1992 - 53.2 days(2100/14400 x 365)

g) **Debt/equity ratio** = $\dfrac{\text{Long-term loans}}{\text{Shareholders' funds}}$

This shows the degree to which the company depends on outside finance, e.g. banks, to run its business. A high D/E ratio may therefore mean high interest charges which could reduce profit. On the other hand, if the company's return on capital is higher than the current interest rates then a high D/E should increase the return on shareholders' funds.
Autotech's Debt/equity ratio =1990 - 8.2% (82:1000)
    1991 - 34% (343:1000)
    1992 - 29.6% (296:1000)

## Answers to questions

1 a) Return on capital 1990 = 2.39%, 1991 = 22.4%, 1992 = 23.6%.
b) Debt/equity ratio 1990 = 8.2 %, 1991 = 34%, 1992 = 29.6 %.
c) Changes in Debtors/Creditors ratio 1990 = 1.16, 1991 = 1.3, 1992 =1.43.
d) Current ratio changes 1990 = 2.14:1, 1991 = 1.62:1, 1992 = 1.60:1.
e) Earnings per share 1990 2.8p, 1991 24p, 1992 40p.

2 Because Autotech's debt/equity ratio is already around 30%, the ability to finance further expansion through long-term loans may be restricted. For this reason, the flotation of a proportion of the company's shares on the stock market may be advisable. Students should also consider whether £18m will be enough to finance the planned expansion. If turnover expanded to £200m p.a., much more than this sum would be required to finance new plant and working capital. If this were the case, the bank may well advise the company to look for a joint venture partner.

## Target student commentary

Autotech's recent expansion has been financed by an increase of both equity and bank loans although the latter have increased more than proportionately. The debt/equity ratio now stands at about 30%. This has probably allowed the company to increase its return to shareholders since the current Return on capital employed is 24% which is probably considerably above current interest rates. However, it would seem that the company is approaching its limits as far as further bank loans are concerned. The company's liquidity seems satisfactory and, although its collection period has increased, this has been offset to some extent by an increased Creditors ratio. Overall, the balance sheet and P & L accounts indicate a satisfactory state of affairs for the company.

# Page 57 Meeting!

Students discuss the best way to raise the new funds either as a continuation of the case study or as members of the Autotech and Hunter-Benson teams.

## Hunter-Benson options

### Language objective

1 Discussing the pros and cons of the different methods of finance, e.g. *The problem with further loans is the additional interest payments.*
2 Advising and recommending in a financial context, e.g. *We would advise you to float a proportion of your shares on the stock exchange.*
3 Arguing for a financial strategy on the basis of financial statements and marketing/production targets, e.g. *With your technical record you could raise sufficient funds through further loans and a public share issue.*

### Notes

1 **Roll-over loan** A bank loan renewed at regular periods according to needs and repayment schedules. Advantage = flexible. Disadvantage = expensive.
2 **Eurobond market** Cash raised through international banks with a fixed rate of interest. Advantage = may be less expensive. Disadvantage = lengthy process.
3 **Joint venture** Set up a company in association with another company i.e. shared ownership. Advantage = reduced investment/shared risk. Disadvantage = loss of control/reduced profit because shared.
4 **Private share sale** Sale of some shares to a chosen partner. Advantage = choice of partner. Disadvantage = difficult to assess correct price of share/loss of control.
5 **Stock exchange flotation** Sale of shares to public. Advantage = could raise large sums if public sees shares as a good buy. Disadvantage = loss of control.
6 **Licence** Sell permission to produce product to another company. Advantage = reduced investment and risk. Disadvantage = transfers competitive advantage to competitor.

## Simulation

Students have to consider the possibilities of raising £18m or more through one or a combination of the above methods. There are several factors in the company's favour:
a) Its current Return on capital employed.
b) Its record of successful expansion so far.
c) Its excellent R&D record.
d) Its new product.
e) The potential market for the new product.

### The Autotech team

The Autotech team should be told to familiarize themselves with market, product and production situation of Autotech as outlined in Unit 10. The financial expert on the team should also analyze the company's financial statements on pages 55 and 56 and explain their main points to the other members of the team. Finally, the team should devise a presentation plan for the meeting with the merchant bank. Their aim is to present their plans and the financial needs to achieve their targets to the bankers.

### The bank team

This team should not necessarily be exposed to the background of Autotech as given in Unit 10 but should elicit this information during the opening stages of the meeting from the Autotech team. Their main preparation should be a detailed analysis of the Autotech financial statements together with a discussion of the options open to raise the new capital. They should listen to the presentation by the Autotech team and be prepared to question them on all its aspects. Their final target should be to devise a plan of action which will allow the company to go into the new market.

## Likely outcome

If the estimated turnover after the launch of the Mk 2 is in excess of £100m p.a., the company is likely to need more than £18m of new capital. For this reason, the bank may be cautious and suggest a collaborative deal with, for example, one of the automobile manufacturers. In this situation, the bank may be willing to make a loan to finance Autotech's part of such a deal. If, on the other hand, the bank thought that Autotech's excellent financial record, together with its new product, would appeal to stock market investors, it may recommend a share flotation.

# Unit 12 Agrichem International

## Synopsis

This unit is about evaluating and selecting an overseas distributor and then negotiating terms of business with that distributor. Agrichem, a European manufacturer of agricultural chemicals, receives a complaint about its present distributor in Ecuador. After checking the distributor's performance in recent years, the company decides to look for a replacement.

## Case objectives

1 Assessing the performance of an agent or distributor in an overseas country.
2 Selecting a new distributor from a short list of candidates.
3 Negotiating an agreement with the selected distributor.

## Overall language objectives

1 Describing the performance of an overseas distributor.
2 Discussing the qualities that make a good distributor.
3 Negotiating an agreement.

## Suggested preparation

Ask students to explain the difference between an agent and a distributor. Elicit or provide the following distinction:

An *agent* (or commissioned representative) usually takes no financial risk and is paid a commission by the manufacturer based on sales.

A *distributor* assumes financial risk by buying the product on his own account from the manufacturer and selling at an agreed list price, taking profit from the difference between the buying and selling prices. Note that there is often confusion between the terms agent and distributor.

You should ensure that students have studied and practised the language of meetings and negotiations (See pages viii and ix) before starting the simulation on page 61.

## Classroom management

This unit divides into three parts: evaluation of Agrichem's present distributor on pages 58 and 59, selection of a replacement distributor on page 60 and negotiations with the new distributor on pages 61 to 63. A case study approach is taken on pages 58 and 59, and a simulation approach on pages 60 and 61 to 63.

For students wishing to take part in the negotiating simulation only, pages 58 to 60 may be used as a brief warm-up and background to the negotiations.

# Page 58
# Agrichem International

Students read the background on the company, listen to a telephone conversation in which a customer complains and study a map of Agrichem's supply routes and operations in Ecuador.

## The telephone call to Head Office

### Language objectives

1 Identifying the problems the customer is having in Ecuador.
2 Noting some of the standard communicative exponents of a business telephone conversation.

### Target lexis

| | | |
|---|---|---|
| regional director | requirement | exploration well |
| supply | contacts | to neglect |
| quantity | Amazon basin | |

See page 85 of the *Student's Book* for the tapescript.

### Answers to questions

2 Sanchez cannot get enough Martox insecticide when he wants it.
3 Dr. Núñez, the owner of Biopharm, is more interested in his other business activities, for example, oil exploration.

### Further questions

1 What is Sanchez's good news?
*His company is standardized on Martox.*
2 How much Martox does Sanchez require immediately?
*10,000 litres.*

### Target student commentary

It is clear that Agrichem's present distributor in Ecuador is not performing well. A major customer has been unable to get supplies and is unhappy. The main reason for this seems to be that the distributor has interests in oil exploration which are causing him to neglect Agrichem's business in the country.

## Map of Agrichem operations in Ecuador

### Language objectives

1 Describing the general logistics of getting products to world markets, e.g. *The product has to be shipped via Panama to Guayaquil.*
2 Summarizing the structure of an overseas distributorship, e.g. *Biopharm consists of the owner, two technical salesmen, one clerk and a secretary.*
3 Describing the overall market in which a distributor operates, e.g. *Ecuador exports almost $240m worth of bananas each year.*

### Answers to questions

2 Agrichem sells two kinds of products in Ecuador. It sells insecticides through Biopharm and it sells industrial chemicals through a separate distributor.
3 Ecuador's total exports amount to $2.393 billion of which half is oil. Bananas represent 10% of exports and these exports are rising at 15% a year.

### Further questions

1 What is the delivery time for Martox Y from the manufacturer to the distributor?
*2 months.*
2 How many litres of Martox Y did Biopharm sell in the current year?
*64,800.*

### Target student commentary

Agrichem sells two main products in Ecuador in two very different kinds of markets. It uses specialist distributors for each product. Martox is used mainly on banana plantations and, since exports of bananas are expanding at 15% p.a.,the market for Martox should also be expanding.

---

# Page 59  The Ecuador File

Students compare Biopharm's performance over the last four years against regional banana production and Martox usage per hectare.

## Agrichem South America File Ecuador

### Language objectives

1 Detecting and describing trends from a table or chart, e.g. *There has been a switch from Gros Michel to Cavendish bananas.*

2 Interpreting the situation depicted on a table, e.g. *It would seem that Cavendish bananas are a more productive type of banana.*
3 Making recommendations on the basis of information available, e.g. *The main target should be to reach the South American average of 3.9 litres per hectare.*

### Target lexis

| | | |
|---|---|---|
| table | to switch to | intensive |
| planted hectares | productive | trend |
| litres per hectare | usage | penetration |
| to swing to | application rate | to lag behind |

### Answers to questions

2 In recent years there has been a switch from Gros Michel to Cavendish bananas. This has been accompanied by a decrease in the total planted area but an increase of 72% in total exports of bananas. This suggests that the Cavendish banana is a more productive type, although, at the same time, the increase in the use of Martox may suggest that the new banana is more susceptible to disease.
3 Biopharm's figure of 1.05 litres of Martox per planted hectare is much lower than the 3.9 litre average for other South American distributors. This suggests that Martox penetration in Ecuador is lagging seriously behind other countries. This means either that the use of insecticides in Ecuador is low or that competing products have a much higher share of the Ecuadorian market.

### Further questions

1 How many litres of Martox could Biopharm sell if it achieved the average South American penetration of 3.9 litres per hectare?
*257,000 litres, i.e. 66,000 hectares x 3.9 litres per hectare.*
2 Where has Biopharm failed?
*It has failed to persuade the plantations to use more litres of Martox Y per hectare.*

### Target student commentary

Biopharm has obviously failed to exploit the Ecuadorian market by increasing the application rate of Martox by farmers. While the average per hectare in South America is 3.9 litres, Biopharm achieved only 1.05 litres in Ecuador. This represents a serious lack of market penetration for which the distributor must take much of the blame. Agrichem can clearly expect a target figure for Martox far in excess of Biopharm's present 64,800 litres p.a.

# Page 60 **Goodbye Dr Núñez. Hello Sr...?**

Students read that Agrichem has decided to buy itself out of the contract with Biopharm. They then listen to Agrichem's Thompson and Mathison discussing the qualities that an effective distributor in Ecuador would need. Students then hold a meeting as A.I. employees to select the best potential distributor from a short list of three. You could stay with the case study approach at this point.

## Mathison and Thompson's discussion

### Language objective

Listening for and reporting the arguments for and against particular qualities in a distributor, e.g. *Thompson argues that energy and enthusiasm are more important than an established distribution system.*

### Target lexis

| | |
|---|---|
| enthusiasm | to be committed to |
| link | ideal |
| to sweat blood for | conflict of interest |
| on paper | track record |
| gap | capital |
| expertise | life blood |
| connections | to adapt |
| to have someone in mind | |

See page 85 of the *Student's Book* for the tapescript.

### Answers to questions

2 Established distribution systems would be useful but enthusiasm, energy and commitment are probably more important as the case of Biopharm demonstrates. A track record in agrochemicals may not be so important as technical expertise can be provided.

### Target student commentary

Thompson disagrees with Mathison's cautious approach to the selection of a replacement distributor for Núñez. He is looking for an energetic individual with a record of quick growth in business but not necessarily in agrochemicals. He believes that Agrichem can supply the necessary product expertise. Mathison, on the other hand, thinks they should look for an established distributor. Thompson thinks this may cause conflicts of interest and cause a lack of commitment to the product.

## Short list

### Language objectives

1 Summarizing the strengths and weaknesses of candidates, e.g. *Royce-Martínez's main weakness is that they have no product knowledge. On the other hand, they have an excellent growth record.*
2 Making and justifying recommendations on the basis of available facts, e.g. *I would recommend Royce-Martínez because of ...*

## Meeting simulation

**Grunwald**
Advantages: established agrochemical distributor; good product knowledge; good management; good distribution system; financially sound.
Disadvantages: partly owned by one of Agrichem's competitors; distributes for another competitor; not clear why they want Martox.

**Mercator**
Advantages: they understand the needs of the market; excellent political connections; already account for 23% of Martox sales in Ecuador; good management and finance. Disadvantages: main interest is banana growing; no sales experience; uncertainty about motives for diversification.

**Royce-Martínez**
Advantages: record of quick growth; already distributes AI's industrial chemicals; keen to diversify because of market growth.
Disadvantages: it is a small company; it is a young company; it has no product knowledge; it has no distribution system for agrochemicals.

## Likely outcome

Any deal with Grunwald may involve conflicts of interest and there are also question marks against its motives for wanting to sell Martox Y. Mercator is primarily a banana grower and has no experience of selling agrochemicals. Royce-Martínez, on the other hand, is a young, dynamic company which, although it has no expertise in agrochemicals, has a good track record in its own field. Agrichem knows that a lot depends on individuals and this may cause them to select Royce-Martínez.

# Negotiation!

Students take the roles of Group 1, Agrichem, and Group 2, the new distributor. They then study their position papers (Agrichem on page 61 and the distributor on page 62) and prepare their negotiating strategies. In a 1:1 situation you may take one of the roles.

## Group 1 Agrichem position paper
### Note
F.O.B. = free on board. This means the cost of goods up to the point they arrive at the loading docks.
C.I.F. = cost, insurance, freight. This means the cost of carrying goods to the final port of destination.
Product registration = any product which may be potentially hazardous, e.g. drugs, agrochemicals, have to be registered officially in the countries where they will be used and tested by those countries for suitability.

### Negotiating points to note
**Clause 1** Biopharm already sells 64,800 litres at 1.05 litres per hectare. If this were increased to the South American average of 3.9 l.p.h., that figure could rise to over 200,000 litres p.a.
**Clause 2** 40,000 litres opening stock would represent about three months' sales, i.e. about 24% of annual sales. Since delivery time ex-Antwerp is 2 months, this would be a safe stock to hold.
**Clause 3** This will allow a potential margin per litre of $3.82.
**Clauses 4-7** These are all self-evident.
**Clause 8** This will ensure a strong management team.
**Clause 9** This will be an important confidence-building gesture.
**Clauses 10-11** These are necessary in the light of past experience.

This position paper is clearly only a starting point for negotiations and Agrichem must be realistic about the chances of raising sales to this level in the first year. It may also have to help the distributor to finance such a large opening stock. The company may also find that a price of $7 per litre is over-optimistic since competition is probably keen. A lower price would alter the distributor's margins and increase cash flow problems. The potential distributor is also likely to object to the lack of options for other AI products and also the very severe contract termination clauses. AI, of course, may not in the end wish to have a distributor and may wish to set up a direct subsidiary itself.

## Group 2 position paper
### Negotiating points to note
**Clause 1** 30% above Biopharm sales levels, i.e. 10% natural rise + 20% effort, would be a good result for the first year, i.e. about 84,000 litres.
**Clause 2** Because of competition anything over $5 would be risky.
**Clause 3** AI's 120 day credit period is effectively only 60 days because of the 60 days transit from Antwerp. With the typical 160-240 payment period of customers in Ecuador, distributor may have to finance stocks from 180 days upwards, i.e. 240 − 60 = 180.
**Clause 4** Agrichem must help to finance the lengthy collection period.
**Clauses 5-6** Contract periods must be realistic to get the company on its feet.
**Clauses 7-9** Incentives must be built into the agreements.
The potential distributor has got to be cautious about sales targets in the first year. Many things could happen after a change of distributorship. In addition to this it must take a realistic view of prices. The most likely price per litre is $6 but it could go lower if competition is fierce. Perhaps the major problem is the debtor/creditor payment situation. At the moment it will pay after 60 days of receiving goods and collect up to 240 days after sale. That means it may need at least 180 days of working capital. It will have to arrange this capital either through banks or through AI. The company certainly wishes to have options on other AI products and will need an annually renewable three year contract in order to establish itself effectively and look to the long term rather than worry about short-term problems with its supplier. It also thinks an incentive discount from AI would be beneficial to both sides.

## Capital needed
## Rough profit and loss account

### Target student commentary
These figures assume a very low starting stock and a relatively low debtor figure. The final Year 1 profit represents only 18.5% return on capital which is only a little above current rates of interest in Ecuador. However, these are first year figures and companies do not expect to become really profitable until, say, the third year of operation. Even so, any improvement on rough figures which can be gained during the negotiations will help.

# Page 63 Simulation

Students take part in a simulated negotiation and fill in their agreement on the grid provided.

**Group 1** Agrichem should present its opening position on the basis of the position paper on page 61.

**Group 2** The new distributor should present its opening position on the basis of the position paper on page 62, supported by the figures at the bottom of the page.

The progress of the negotiations will vary according to the student groups but below are some of the concessions that may be made:

1 Opening stock of 40,000 litres required by AI could be reduced or AI could offer to finance that stock.

2 Credit period of 120 days could be extended to, say, 180 days on the first shipment.

3 AI could help the distributor to improve collection systems and thus reduce the number of debtors.

4 AI could put up 20% of the initial capital or give 8 months' credit for the first three years.

5 AI could agree to a lower sales target for Year 1 but rising quickly over Year 2 and 3.

6 AI could give a growth rebate of, say, 10% of F.O.B. price on all purchases over a certain agreed figure.

7 AI could provide a technical manager and general manager free of charge for three years.

## Final agreement between Agrichem and the new distributor

### Possible outcome

There is no one agreement for this negotiation but the following outcome is feasible:

| | |
|---|---|
| Sales targets, Year 1 | 100,000 ltrs |
| Sales targets, Year 2 | 170,000 ltrs |
| Sales targets, Year 3 | 240,000 ltrs |
| Credit terms (days) | 180 days (Yrs 1 & 2). 120 days |
| Capital injection | $50,000 for three years. |
| Other | First refusal on other AI Agrichem products |

| | |
|---|---|
| Selling price | $6 |
| Buying price | $3.18 |
| Discounts | 10% on sales over targets |
| Opening stock | 30,000 ltrs |
| Personnel | AI to provide one technical manager and one General Manager at 50% cost. |
| Contract period | Three years + annual review + one year's notice of termination. |

# Unit 13 Our man in Nam Doa

## Synopsis

This unit focusses upon personnel problems related to foreign assignments. Scanco, a Swedish company, sends one of its best technical managers to a remote location in South East Asia to oversee the installation of a wood crushing unit. A few weeks after the manager's arrival in the country, the company's project coordinator in the capital receives news that the manager has gone missing. The project coordinator has to decide how to react in both the short- and the long-term.

## Case objectives

1 Finding out why an overseas executive assignment went wrong.
2 Deciding how to react to a crisis in an overseas project.
3 Devising a system for establishing and monitoring the personnel aspects of overseas executive assignments.

## Overall language objectives

1 Identifying and discussing the psychological and motivational problems of personnel on overseas assignments.
2 Reporting and interpreting various forms of business communications, e.g. telex messages, letters.
3 Making recommendations for an overseas personnel policy.

## Suggested preparation

Ask students what special terms they would wish to have in their contracts if their company asked them to work overseas, e.g. increase in salary, subsistence allowance, gratuity, regular return fares to their own countries and language training. Ask them to consider what the problems of working abroad might be.

## Classroom management

This unit adopts a case study approach throughout although it could be concluded with a simulation in which the Scanco Managing Director, Lars Arlbjorg, and the project coordinator, Jan Berling, meet each other to sort out the Nam Doa problem and to devise a new personnel policy to prevent a recurrence of the situation.

---

## Page 64
## Our man in Nam Doa

---

Students read a telex and then study the background to Scanco's operations in Nam Doa.

## Telex

### Language objective

Reporting the content of a telex message, e.g. *It says that the project is at a standstill because Wikström has left the site.*

### Target lexis

| | |
|---|---|
| ATTN.= Attention | ASAP = as soon as possible |
| PROJ.= project | RPT = repeat |
| RE: = about | TLX = telex |
| FLT = flight | soonest = as soon as possible |
| RGDS = regards | ETA = estimated time of arrival |
| PLS = please | |

### Answers to questions

2 The project at Nam Doa has come to a standstill although the exact cause is not quite clear. There is a technical problem in the wood crusher unit but it is not clear if this happened before Wikström's departure or after it. The area director, Mr Chao, is obviously worried about the absence of Wikström and wants a replacement and a reply to his telex quickly.

## Background

### Questions

1 Who is Jan Berling and where is he located?
*He is project coordinator for Scanco and is in the capital Ban Hua.*
2 Where is the project situated?
*At Nam Doa, 500 miles north of Ban Hua.*
3 Who is Nils Wikström?
*He is Scanco's Technical Liaison Manager in Nam Doa.*
4 What happened to Wikström's predecessor?
*He was sent home after an incident at an embassy party.*

# Page 65
# A note from Wikström

Students read about the action Berling took on receiving the telex and then discuss a document annotated by Wikström which arrived mysteriously on Berling's desk.

## Scanco conditions of employment

### Language objectives

1 Reading and explaining the formal clauses of employment conditions, e.g. *A gratuity of 20% of gross salary is payable at the completion of the assignment.*
2 Interpreting opinions regarding terms of employment, e.g. *Wikström clearly thinks that the terms of employment do not adequately take into account the difficulties of the job.*
3 Reading between the lines, e.g. *Wikström implies that it is a hardship assignment.*

### Target lexis

| | |
|---|---|
| conditions of employment | gross salary |
| domicile | assignment |
| messing allowance | terminal gratuity |
| clause | to be responsible for |
| to repatriate | duration |
| schooling allowance | supplement |
| to fail to | to fulfil |
| return air fare | |

### Answers to questions

2 The assignments last three years and home salary is increased by 50%. A 20% gratuity will be paid if the employee completes the assignment. In addition to this, there are various allowances including messing and schooling. Single accommodation is provided but the employee will have to make his own arrangements for family accommodation. The employee will have to pay his own return air fare if he terminates the contract prematurely.
3 Wikström is obviously distressed. He finds the site very unpleasant to work in and thinks that the financial compensation is inadequate. He compares his salary with the German site manager and points out that his expenses are insufficient to cover normal expenditure.

# Page 66 Berling calls the Ministry and checks the files

Students listen to a telephone call between Berling and the Ministry and then read a letter from the personnel files about Wikström's character and situation.

## Telephone conversation between Berling and the Ministry

### Language objective

Listening for and reporting the gist of a heavily accented telephone conversation in English.

### Target lexis

| | |
|---|---|
| to get to the bottom of something | foreman |
| to fill someone in | argument |
| at a standstill | to go absent |
| to be behind schedule | |

See page 86 of the *Student's Book* for the tapescript.

### Answers to questions

2 Berling rings the Ministry to clarify the situation at Nam Doa. Mr Dong tells him that Wikström was involved in a fight with a foreman. The fight started as an argument about training. Training was part of the contract but Wikström was not a good trainer and he made people angry. Mr Dong also brought up the subject of Mrs Wikström. She is still in Nam Doa and is running language courses for the workers. Berling says that he will fly there immediately.
3 It seems that Wikström may have had problems of communication with his fellow workers at Nam Doa. He does not seem to have had much patience with them and did not fulfil the training part of his function. There is also some evidence that Mrs Wikström may be part of the problem. As she is still there, the question is, why did she not fly home with her husband? Is she in some way the cause of the problem? It may be that they had some kind of argument.

## Scanco Personnel Division letter

### Language objectives

1 Reading between the lines, e.g. *Wikström's wife is clearly a strong character and may have been a major influence on his decision to go to Nam Doa and on his subsequent behaviour.*
2 Guessing what might have happened, e.g. *It may be that Mrs Wikström persuaded her husband to take the job so that she could travel and work in Asia.*

## Answers to questions

2 Wikström is a quiet, sensitive man with interests in oriental art. This was clearly a factor in his selection. He is also a perfectionist. He accepted the position on the condition that his wife and child could join him. The Personnel Division asked Berling to help them as much as possible.

3 Although Wikström is very intelligent, he is possibly rather introverted and may have problems communicating with other people. It seems as if he was chosen because he was very different from the man who caused the earlier troubles. In other words, he seemed 'safe'. It is also possible that Wikström is considerably influenced by his wife. She is an extrovert character with a lot of ambition. It could be that she persuaded him to accept the job. He may now blame her for some of his troubles. This would explain why he has returned home and she has stayed on.

---

# Page 67 Another telex: Berling prepares for a very important meeting

---

Students study a telex which announces the imminent arrival from Sweden of Berling's Managing Director. They then draw up a series of recommendations for dealing with the problem in the long run and the short run.

## Telex

### Language objective

Reporting the content of a telex, e.g. *The telex says that Scanco's Managing Director will be arriving on the next flight from Sweden.*

### Answers to questions

2 The telex says that Wikström is back in Sweden and is probably blaming Berling for some of his problems. The Ban Hua Ministry is threatening to use the penalty clause and may even cancel the contract. Berling's Managing Director clearly sees this as a major crisis and is flying out to Ban Hua immediately. This is obviously a major career crisis for Berling and he has got to argue his case very well if he wants to keep his job.

## Further questions

1 What reasons does Wikström give for leaving Nam Doa?
*Lack of support; breakdown of morale; communication problems with locals.*
2 What does Wikström say about his wife?
*He said there had been a row.*

## Target student commentary

Wikström's arrival back in Stockholm together with the telex from the Ministry has created a state of crisis in Head Office. It seems that Wikström may be pinning a lot of the blame on Berling and the fact that the Managing Director is flying out points to some serious talking to be done. Berling will obviously have to come up with a good explanation and some ideas about the true causes of the problem and how to prevent this happening again.

## Conclusion of case study

Students now a) analyze the evidence before them, using Berling's notes as an informal agenda, and b) devise a series of recommendations.

As has been stated, an alternative activity would be a 1:1 simulation of a meeting between Berling and Arlbjorg, with Berling fighting to save his career and making recommendations for the future.

### a) Analysis

**1 Recruitment:** Wikström was the wrong man for the job. He has personality and family problems which interfered with his work. The recruitment process was defective. It should have detected these problems in Sweden.

**2 Acclimatization:** There was no training or preparation for this post. Wikström had never worked abroad before and Nam Doa was a very inhospitable location for such a person.

**3 Conditions:** These do not seem to take into account the actual living costs in Nam Doa. They are too general and may not be attractive enough to compensate for the hardships.

**4 Training role:** This part of the contract seems to have been neglected. Wikström was clearly a good technician but a bad trainer. This relates again to the recruitment process. Also, the implied absence of a language training programme shows severe shortcomings in such a project.

**5 Role of project coordinator:** Clearly Berling had little influence in the selection of staff for Nam Doa.

**6 Wikström's wife:** She may have done Scanco a service by showing up the defects in the system, e.g. the need for more careful screening of staff and families.

**7 Recommendations:** See below.

**b) Possible recommendations**

**1 Recruitment:** Identify the problems associated with overseas assignments, e.g. culture shock, language problems, loneliness and build up an ideal personality profile against which candidates may be measured.

**2 Acclimatization:** Set up training and acclimatization courses in which problems are anticipated and employees prepared for work abroad.

**3 Conditions:** Assess the precise costs and hardship factors on a site-by-site basis and ensure that compensation is adequate.

**4 Training role:** All overseas turnkey projects will need adequate staff training built into them. In Nam Doa there may be a case for appointing a specialist trainer.

**5 Role of project coordinator:** Involve this person more closely in the preparation of the conditions and recruitment policy and selection.

**6 Wives:** Involve wives in the selection process and brief them with their husbands about such assignments.

# Unit 14  Sea link

## Synopsis

This unit is an exercise in project appraisal. The governments of Grunland and Latonia have agreed to build a fixed link across the Western Channel which separates their two countries. Four consortia put forward different proposals. The governments have to select the best proposal against the following criteria:
- financial viability
- technical feasibility
- safety and security
- impact on employment
- political factors
- environmental factors

## Case objectives

1 Devising a list of criteria with the aim of evaluating business proposals.
2 Carrying out an appraisal of different proposals.
3 Calculating the commercial feasibility of different proposals in terms of revenue, costs and payback periods.
4 Making a formal presentation of a technical and commercial proposal.
5 Selecting the best proposal and justifying the decision.

## Language objectives

1 Presenting technical descriptions of proposed projects.
2 Presenting a commercial case for a proposed project.
3 Examining specific business proposals using question and answer techniques.
4 Taking part in a meeting to appraise and discuss the merits and demerits of competing proposals.
5 Presenting a formal decision and its justification.

## Suggested preparation

If time is limited, the information on pages 68 and 69 can be given to students as preparatory homework.

Ask students to think of the various land gaps around the world, e.g. the Channel, the Straits of Gibraltar, the Bering Straits that either have been or could be bridged in the interests of the countries on both sides of the water. Elicit the various methods of creating a fixed link. Indicate that this unit is about appraising different proposals for such a project.

## Classroom management

This unit divides naturally into three stages: the problem - pages 68 and 69, the proposals - pages 70 and 71, and the decision - page 72. There are two possible approaches to this unit. It may be approached as a case study throughout or it can be done as a simulation after pages 68 and 69 with students taking the roles of the representatives of the governments and consortia concerned. The government representatives could present the problem and the requirements for the bids using the information on pages 68 and 69. Following this, formal presentations could be made by each consortium using the information on pages 70 and 71. Finally, the government could invite the four consortia to a round table discussion of the proposals using the additional information from page 72. At the end of the meeting, the government could announce its decision.

---

# Page 68  Sea link

---

Students read about the proposed fixed link.

## Go-ahead for cross-channel link

### Language objectives

1 Identifying and reporting the salient points in an article, e.g. *The most important commercial point is that the project must be self-financing.*
2 Listing and discussing the criteria upon which to judge a business proposal, e.g. *Safety and security are important factors.*

### Answers to questions

2 The project must be self-financing.
3 Safety and security, unemployment, the attitudes of interest groups, the political impact.

### Target student commentary

The governments have approved the fixed link on one important condition, that the project is self-financing. This means that any link must be commercially viable and not supported by government funds. Other factors, too, will be important. The impact on employment and the attitudes of interest groups will be taken into account. There will probably also be political considerations.

# Page 69 **The problem**

Students study the route of the proposed link, discuss the problems that have to be overcome and assess its commercial potential.

## Proposed route of the Western Channel fixed link map

### Language objectives

1 Describing transport routes, e.g. *The existing ferry routes carry 10 million passengers a year between Grunland and Latonia.*
2 Identifying and explaining the technical problems posed by an engineering project, e.g. *Any structure would have to withstand wind speeds of up to 120 k.p.h.*
3 Calculating and presenting revenue forecasts from existing routes, e.g. *Existing passenger revenues on the ferries amount to $330m per annum.*

### Target lexis

| | | |
|---|---|---|
| ferry | geology | outcrop |
| return fare | sandstone | prevailing wind |
| coach | sedimentary deposits | incident |
| lorry | granite | to withstand |

### Answers to questions

2 The main problems are granite outcrops, strong winds, fog and ice, the danger of collisions and competition from the existing ferry services.
3 Revenues from existing air and ferry services amount to $674m per annum ($330m passengers + $ 65m cars + $48m coaches + $75m lorries + $56m air). It is difficult to know what share of this traffic the fixed link could expect. A 75% market share would give it revenues of $505.5m p.a. This would have to cover all operating costs and provide a return on overhead investment sufficient to attract investors.

### Target student commentary

The Western Channel is a major shipping route which already has an accident problem. The cross-channel traffic is very heavy and the number of major and minor accidents per annum points to a considerable safety problem. On the commercial side, the cross-channel routes generate $674m revenue per annum. The difficult geology and weather conditions will have to be taken into account in any project appraisal.

# Pages 70 and 71 **The bids**

Students study the proposals of the four consortia and compare their advantages and disadvantages. Alternatively, students can take the roles of representatives of the two governments and the four consortia with the latter making presentations of their projects.

For students adopting a case study approach, a grid containing the main criteria could be drawn up to compare each proposal. The grid could be based on the items listed at the bottom of each of the consortia diagrams. Students could discuss and agree this grid and then allocate the proposals to individuals for appraisal. Students wishing to calculate a simple payback period could use the formula below for this calculation:

$$PB = \frac{TC}{TR - OC} + PC$$

where PB = payback period, TC = total cost of construction, TR = total revenue per year, OC = operating cost per year and PC = period of construction.

If time allows, students should be encouraged to make their own payback calculations in order to maximize their involvement in the unit. If time is short, these figures could be presented to the students. The approximate payback periods, assuming revenues based on the relevant five year forecasts and a 50% market share, are:

Bridge: 5.9 years
Brunnel: 10 years
Tunnel 11.25 years
Super-ferry 3.4 years

Note that the Super-ferry project payback period could be shorter than 3.4 years as the project consists of a fleet rather than one ship, i.e. the first ships delivered will be generating revenue before the last ship is delivered.

Note also that all the above payback calculations may be improved on if students think that their proposal is so superior that it could charge higher prices for its service without significantly damaging its market share. Other factors which could influence the calculations are a) What proportion of the existing traffic will transfer to the fixed link? b) Will existing ferry operators undercut a fixed link to maintain market share? c) How realistic are the consortia forecasts?

For students adopting a simulation approach, the same calculations should be made or provided for use in their presentations to the governments of Latonia and Grunland.

# The four consortia

## Language objectives

1 Presenting an overview of the main technical features of a project, e.g. *The Brunnel proposal consists of bridge sections over the outcrops and a tunnel section in mid-channel.*
2 Describing the technical advantages and disadvantages of a project, e.g. *The main technical advantage of the Brunnel proposal is that it has the safety of a tunnel while avoiding the problems of the granite outcrops.*
3 Making presentations of the commercial features of a project, e.g. *Our forecasts show a 35% traffic increase over the next five years which would mean total available revenues of £910m per year.*

## The Bridge Consortium

### Target lexis

| | | |
|---|---|---|
| disruption | to suspend | operating costs |
| running costs | aerodynamic tube | congestion |
| to ventilate | to drill | hazard |
| motorway | | |

### Answers to questions

1 The bridge is a direct road link which means that, unlike the tunnel, drivers and passengers do not have to leave their cars and there is a minimum of congestion at the terminals. It also has the second fastest journey time. The bridge will not involve expensive drilling through the granite. But there will be a series of towers and these could represent a hazard to shipping.
2 The cost of construction is $2.3bn which makes it cheaper than the other fixed links. It can also be built more quickly. On the employment side, it creates the fewest permanent jobs although 130,000 temporary jobs will be created during construction. Its operating costs are very low at $50m per annum and, if its traffic forecasts are correct, the payback period on investment would be roughly 6 years, depending on its share of the total cross-channel revenues. The downside forecast is a 50% share. So present total revenues $674m + 30% = $876m x 50% = £438m annual revenue. Less operating costs of $50m = net contribution to payback of $388m p.a. Total investment = $2.3bn ÷ $388m = 5.9 years.

### Target student commentary

The main advantages of the bridge project are its low cost, speed of construction and the simple method of transportation involved. Its low running costs will allow the investment to be recouped quickly at the same time as allowing reasonable charges to the users. The disadvantage is that the bridge would cross a very busy shipping lane and therefore be vulnerable to damage, especially in fog. In military and strategic terms the bridge would also be vulnerable to terrorists and to hostile armies.

## The Brunnel Group

### Target lexis

| | | |
|---|---|---|
| safety | access | congestion |
| security | free port facilities | trench |
| submersible tube | | |

### Answers to questions

2 The Brunnel proposal is a road system consisting of bridge sections over the granite outcrops leading to island terminals. At these points the road enters a tunnel which leads to the opposite island terminal. The tunnel section is prefabricated and laid into a trench on the sea bed rather than drilled through rock as in the tunnel project. The main technical advantage of the Brunnel system is that it does not create a hazard to shipping and does not involve expensive drilling through granite.
3 The cost of construction is $3.6bn for the non-rail tunnel version. This means that it is more expensive than the bridge but less expensive than the tunnel. It creates more permanent jobs than either of the other fixed links and also creates 80,000 temporary jobs during construction. Its period of construction is 4.5 years. Its operating costs are higher than the other fixed links. If its traffic forecasts are correct, it will have a payback period of between five and ten years, i.e. $674m + 35 % = $910m x 50% (downside market share) = $455m. With operating costs of £100m p.a., the net contribution to investment = $355m. Total investment = $3.6bn. Thus maximum payback period = $3.6bn ÷ 355m = 10 years.

### Target student commentary

The Brunnel proposal is an attempt to combine the advantages of the bridge and tunnel while avoiding their disadvantages. The bridge sections will allow quick access to the link and avoid the need to bore a tunnel through the granite outcrops. The tunnel section will allow free and safe passage for shipping and thus avoid the high accident risk of a single bridge. Another feature of this proposal is the concept of the island terminals. These will prevent environmental damage and congestion on the mainland and also offer excellent free port facilities.

## The Tunnel Group

### Target lexis

viable      shuttle service
troublefree      to bore
twin-bore

### Answers to questions

2 This is a railway tunnel only. Road traffic transfers to railway carriages at the mainland terminals and is carried quickly through the tunnel. The service is safe and avoids weather and shipping problems. It is the fastest method of transport proposed.

3 The total cost of construction is $4.5bn which makes it the most expensive of all the proposals. It will also take longer than the other projects to complete. On the jobs front, it will create a relatively low number of permanent jobs. Its operating costs are $90m p.a. If its traffic forecasts are correct, it will have a payback period of 11.25 years. Present market = $674m + 45% = $977m x 50% (downside market share forecast) = $489m. With operating costs of $90m p.a., it will have a net contribution towards investment of $399m p.a. With total costs of $4.5bn, this will give a payback period of 11.25 years.

### Target student commentary

The tunnel is the most costly proposal and will require the longest period of construction. But it probably represents the safest and most secure system since it will not be subject to weather conditions, will not be a shipping hazard, will be more secure against military or terrorist attack and will not be subject to the high accident risks of a car driver based system. The tunnel is also the fastest method of transportation and will allow drivers and passengers to relax during the crossing. Its final advantage is that it will allow a direct rail link between Grunland and Latonia with a rapid transit of goods.

## The Super-ferry Consortium

### Target lexis

flexible      optimistic
proven      to be at risk
capacity

### Answers to questions

2 This project is not a fixed link but an extension of the existing ferry service through the building of larger and more economical ferries.

3 The total cost of building a fleet of new super-ferries is $500m. The period of construction is only 2.5 years. Present permanent jobs will be saved and these will increase at 2% p.a. The consortium believes that traffic will increase by 20% in five years and that all other forecasts are optimistic. Operating costs are great, though. If forecasts are correct, then the payback period on investment will be between four and nine years, i.e. $674m + 20% = $809m x 50% = $405m. Deduct the operating costs of $250m p.a. = net contribution to the overhead investment of $155m p.a. The payback period = 3.4 years.

### Target student commentary

The Super-ferry consortium believes that an expansion of the existing ferry system will be in the best interests of both countries. It will ensure the lowest fares for passengers and involve the minimum outlay of capital. In addition to this, the port infrastructure already exists and the current employment situation will not worsen. The group also believes that the other consortia are being over-optimistic in their passenger traffic forecasts in order to improve their profitability forecasts.

---

# Page 72
# An historic opportunity

Students study four newspaper clippings about the fixed link and then take part in a round table discussion to select the best proposal or proceed with the simulation in which the governments call a meeting with the representatives of the four consortia to discuss the proposals and reach a decision.

## The four newspaper articles

### Answers to questions

**Residents of Latonia demand public enquiry**

2 Job losses in the ferry industry; damage to the local environment and wildlife due to the building of new terminals. This indicates strong lobby pressure against any fixed link.

**Protest demonstration against Channel link**

2 Damage to Grunland's national culture and heritage due to the link with Latonia. Clearly, nationalist feeling on both sides of the Channel must be taken into account.

**Rabies scare over fixed link**

2 The threat of the spread of rabies from Latonia to Grunland via the fixed link. Such fears will obviously be used by lobby groups, e.g. the Super-ferry consortium, to support their case against a fixed link.

**Claustrophobia article**

2 The possibility of dangerous psychological reactions among drivers who have to drive through long tunnels. Fear of the unknown is a powerful weapon in a pressure group's armoury.

## Likely outcome

**a) Commercial criteria:** In terms of a payback period and short-term commercial viability, the most attractive proposals are the Super-ferry and the Bridge. But the Super-ferry is not a fixed link and the Bridge has many technical factors against it. Although the Tunnel and Brunnel proposals have long payback periods, these must be judged against the likely life of such infrastructure projects. If the life is fifty years, an 11.25 year payback does not seem quite so long. If students take a long-term view, the final choice could be between the Brunnel and the Tunnel proposals.

**b) Technical and other non-commercial criteria:** All the projects are technically feasible although some face more construction problems than others. Safety with regard to shipping is a major factor against the Bridge, the Super-ferry and even the Brunnel proposal. The Tunnel is faster and safer than the other projects and also has less impact on the environment.

**c) Economic and political criteria:** The influence of these considerations on the final decision will depend on students' interpretation of the governments' viewpoints. The hint of future elections in the article on page 68 may mean that the governments will favour a project with a short construction period and maximum short-term impact on employment. If this were the case, the Bridge proposal would be very attractive. But there is also the lobby pressure from the railways which would be against the Bridge and the Super-ferry bids and the Brunnel proposal in its initial form.

The final choice is likely to be the Tunnel although in the simulation, where students may be able to invent further political complications, any result is possible.

## The tower

### Synopsis

Although this activity derives its storyline from *Pause for thought 4 The oil rig*, it may also be used as a freestanding activity. It requires the use of a set of 300 standard Lego bricks for each group taking part in the activity. The activity involves the scoring of the final structures against the three score charts below. Using the bricks provided, students have to build the highest possible tower, using the minimum number of bricks in the shortest time possible. The students with the highest score win the contract.

### Suggested exploitation

1 Ask the students to read the introduction. Check comprehension.
2 Ask the students to read the tender document. Check understanding of the target activity and rules.
3 Divide the students into groups and allocate 300 lego bricks to each group.
4 Announce the scoring schedules, i.e. there is a maximum of 30 points each for speed of construction and the height of the tower. There is a maximum of 20 points for the number of bricks used. Each parameter will be measured against a fixed graph. These graphs may be handed out if appropriate. Tell students that it is possible to lose points as well as win them. The maximum possible score is 80 points.
5 Give the students a set time for the planning of their towers, e.g. 30 minutes. Tell each group to organize itself and experiment.
6 Ask each group to contruct its tower. As they do this, time them and score them on the following graphs.
7 Announce the winner and present the contract.

**Note**

Most students seem to build their structures from a very broad base in order to give stability to the highest tower possible. The ornamentation of the towers also seems to vary from group to group. However, with a little bit of pre-construction experimentation, students will find that the tower can be built as a simple pile of single bricks, such is the stability of the bricks. This simple solution is often lost on sophisticated business students.

The Government of Vitrasia scoring schedules for the Tower Project.

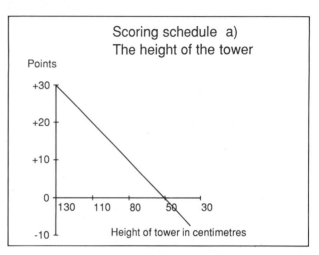

Scoring schedule a)
The height of the tower

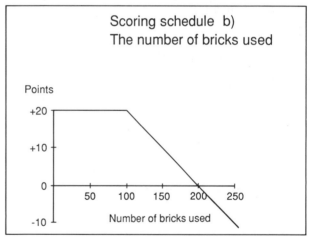

Scoring schedule b)
The number of bricks used

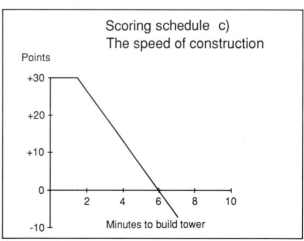

Scoring schedule c)
The speed of construction

# Unit 15 Chun and the desktop computer

## Synopsis

This case is about choosing the right kind of sales and distribution structure for a new product. Chun is a Korean manufacturer of electronic typewriters who has sold his products successfully in the U.K. market through office equipment wholesalers and retailers. Now he has developed a desktop computer and has to decide whether to allow his present typewriter distributors to market the new product or to set up a totally new sales system.

## Case objectives

1 Identifying the specialist skills needed to sell computers compared with those needed to sell typewriters.
2 Deciding whether an existing sales organization can upgrade itself to deal with more complex products and, if so, at what cost and to what effect?
3 Identifying the key market sectors for a new product and moulding sales structure accordingly.
4 Devising a marketing plan to reflect new products and new markets.

## Overall language objectives

1 Describing the technical features of a product.
2 Describing a sales structure and its related distribution and technical support systems.
3 Describing customer needs with regard to hi-tech office products.
4 Describing market segments.
5 Arguing a case for and against particular sales and distribution channels.

## Suggested preparation

You could ask students to study the extract from Chun's speech and the advertisement for the new computer on pages 74 and 75 as preparatory homework. With this background, students can enter the main section of the unit, i.e. the choice of sales channels, more quickly.

Alternatively, open the case by asking students if they own or use a personal computer. Then ask them if they would buy one from a typewriter salesman. Ask them to explain their answers, e.g. *I would not because a computer is much more complex than a typewriter.* Lead into unit introduction on page 74.

## Classroom management

This unit adopts a case study approach until page 78 when students take the roles of Chun's existing typewriter dealers and the Chun management team. The dealers have to persuade the Chun management team to accept them as dealers for the new X-1 computer.

## Pages 74 and 75 Chun and the desktop computer

Students read an extract from an address by Chun, describe his business philosophy and then study and present the features of Chun's new desktop computer as shown in the advertisement.

## Extract from the address by Chun

### Language objective

Describing a business philosophy, e.g. *Chun believes in a late starter strategy where you learn from other people's mistakes.*

### Target lexis

to get in on the ground floor
to have a foot in the door
to ignore

pushing and shoving
to be left behind

### Answers to questions

2 Chun believes in waiting for the right moment to enter a market. An early start means high development costs and the risk of failure. A later start means that you can learn from others' mistakes, assess the market very clearly and enter just when the surviving early starters are maximizing their prices and thus becoming vulnerable. Chun believes that low cost, imitative products coming late into a market can be very successful.

## Page 75 Announcing the Chun X-1 Personal computer

### Language objectives

1 Explaining the features and advantages of a technical product, e.g. *The X-1 has the advantage of a printer built into the machine.*
2 Comparing and contrasting a hi-tech product with its competitors, e.g. *The X-1 has the edge on its competitors because its price is not only much lower but all-inclusive.*

72

## Target lexis

| | | |
|---|---|---|
| expandable | floppy disk | modem |
| VDU | state of the art | peripherals |
| megabyte | processor unit | software |
| dot matrix printer | keyboard | |

### Note

VDU = visual display unit, i.e. the screen.
640K RAM = the computing power of the machine expressed in units of memory, i.e. 640,000 bits.
RAM = random access memory. 1K = 1,000
32 bit processor unit = the power of the central 'control room' of the computer.
Dot matrix printer = a printing machine using a series of tiny dots to build up the form of a character on the page.
Modem = a device for receiving and transmitting computer signals and information via the telephone.

### Answers to questions

2 640K RAM; built-in dot matrix printer; modem; advanced central processor unit; colour VDU.
3 The main competitive advantages are the very low price and the all-inclusive features which are normally extras in competing products.

# Page 76 Overheard at the bar of the Markham Hotel

Students listen to two dealers talking about Chun's speech, study Chun's existing dealership structure, look at some market forecasts for personal computers, and finally hear the great man himself.

## Conversation between two dealers talking at the bar of the Markham Hotel

### Language objective

Reporting the gist of a conversation, e.g. *The first dealer is worried that Chun's existing dealers will not get the X-1 business.*

### Target lexis

| | |
|---|---|
| loyalty | to be open |
| to shift | Come off it! |
| exclusivity clause | the right people for the job |
| to imagine things | for goodness sake |
| to play your cards close to your chest | |

See page 86 of the *Student's Book* for the tapescript.

## Answers to questions

2 The first speaker's main concern is that Chun will not give them the X-1 dealerships unless he is convinced that they are the right people for the job. The other speaker is more optimistic.
3 They have made Chun successful in the U.K. Chun owes them his loyalty.

# Chun's typewriter dealership structure

## Language objectives

1 Describing sales and distribution channels for office products, e.g. *Sales to large businesses go through wholesale distributors.*
2 Describing a manufacturer's sales support system, e.g. *Chun provides a technical back-up service to dealers and distributors.*

## Target lexis

| | | |
|---|---|---|
| warehouse | retail | chain |
| dealership | outlet | sales channels |
| wholesale | support | middleman |

### Note

The terms *dealers*, *wholesalers* and *distributors* are often used without distinction in English. This usage is reflected in this unit.

## Answers to questions

2 Chun does not sell direct to end users in the U.K. but channels his typewriters through middlemen. He sells to large businesses through wholesale distributors and to small businesses through office equipment shops and chains. He gives technical support to these companies through five regional centres.

# Forecast sales of personal computers bar chart

## Language objectives

1 Describing the structure and segmentation of a market, e.g. *The personal computer market breaks down into four major segments.*
2 Presenting forecasts in absolute terms, e.g. *Sales to the business sector are expected to rise from 250,000 units next year to 330,000 units in Year 3.*
3 Presenting forecasts in comparative terms, e.g. *The schools sector is forecast to rise much more quickly than the business sector.*

## Target lexis

| | | |
|---|---|---|
| bar chart | forecast | to predict |
| to break down | to expect | price range |

## Answers to questions

3 The market breaks down into four major sectors. At the moment the largest is the business sector but, whereas this will rise steadily over the next three years, other sectors will expand at a much faster rate. The fastest growing sector of all will be the schools sector followed closely by the home and science sectors.

## Target student commentary

The pattern of demand in the personal computer market is changing rapidly. Although it is now dominated by the business sector, by Year 3 the three non-business sectors together will account for almost two thirds of the total market. The fastest growing sector over this period will be the schools sector. This clearly puts a big question mark next to the suitability of the existing dealers to reach this complex market.

## Chun's summing up

### Language objectives

1 Reporting the gist of what has been said, e.g. *Chun says that he wants the dealers to make proposals that will be a fair deal for everyone.*
2 Interpreting what has been said, e.g. *Chun seems to be threatening to withhold the new dealerships from them.*

### Target lexis

| | |
|---|---|
| to make up your mind | proposal |
| to invest | to sleep on it |

See page 86 of the *Student's Book* for the tapescript.

### Answers to questions

2 Chun wants the best possible results across the whole personal computer market. To achieve this he is willing to invest in his present dealers if they can convince him that they are right for the new job. This investment may mean special training or setting-up costs.

---

# Page 77
# Burning the midnight oil

Students study three possible structures for the new distribution channels and decide which would be best for Chun and the dealers.

## The three options

### Language objectives

1 Describing potential sales channel structures, e.g. *Chun could divide his sales outlets into three to serve specialized sectors of the market.*
2 Comparing the advantages and disadvantages of different sales structures, e.g. *Option 3 would mean a much stronger sales effort towards the schools and science market than the other options could offer.*
3 Criticizing a particular sales structure, e.g. *The trouble with all these options is that existing typewriter dealers would be excluded from the two major growth sectors in the market.*

### Target lexis

| | |
|---|---|
| specialized | exclusive |
| wholesaler | government department |
| direct selling organization | High Street store |

### Answers to questions

2 **Business sector:** very competitive; needs multiple visits to win a sale; large after sales back-up resources needed.
**Home sector:** very price sensitive; margins may be low; low margin-high volume approach may be best but this means major stores would be best outlets.
**Schools sector:** very specialized; direct selling needed; also direct selling to government departments will be needed.
**Science sector:** extremely specialized direct selling needed; multiple visits and specialized software support required.
3 They need to understand the basic background to computing in the areas of both hardware and software; they must be able to demonstrate a range of user software, e.g. word processing programmes, accounting programmes; they must be able to handle simple technical problems; they must be able to advise on a range of computer applications for particular customers.
4 The advantages and disadvantages of the three options are outlined below:

### Option 1

**a) Chun**
Advantages: could commission computer specialists to sell to specialist markets with no further training expenses. In the business sector, his existing typewriter dealers would have instant access to existing typewriter customers.
Disadvantages: computer specialists may already sell competing products; uncertain track records; existing typewriter dealers may not be able to adapt to the business computer market.

**b) Dealers**
Advantages: they get full rights to sell the X-1 to their existing typewriter customers.
Disadvantages: they are excluded from the fastest growing sectors of the market, i.e. schools, homes and science.

## Option 2

### a) Chun
Advantages: there would be healthy competition between existing dealers and specialist computer dealers for the business sector; High Street stores would be good outlets for the homes sector.
Disadvantages: there may be conflict between existing dealers and new dealers for business customers which could damage Chun's reputation; no guarantee that specialist dealers could offer the coverage needed for specialist schools and science sectors; exclusion of existing dealers from other sectors may cause resentment and damage typewriter business.

### b) Dealers
Advantages: they would get some of the existing typewriter business customers.
Disadvantages: they would have to compete directly with specialized computer dealers; they are excluded from the fastest growing sectors of the market.

## Option 3

### a) Chun
Advantages: existing typewriter business continues as usual; direct selling to major growth sectors ensures success; existing dealers allowed to compete with specialist computer dealers for the Chun dealerships.
Disadvantages: difficult to assess potential dealers in advance.

### b) Dealers
Advantages: The typewriter business is clearly separated from the computer business but they have a chance to compete with specialists for both the business and homes sectors.
Disadvantages: excluded from growth sectors and competition on the technical side from existing computer specialists is likely to be very fierce.

---

# Page 78
# The future begins here!

---

Students take on the roles of the Chun management team and dealers, and then take part in a meeting at which the dealers present proposals to persuade Chun to accept them as X-1 dealers. Finally, they draw up an outline agreement.

## Language objectives

1 Presenting proposals with a view to winning a dealership, e.g. *I would suggest that, with the right training, we could soon adapt to the more complex products.*
2 Taking part in a meeting at which an overall sales strategy is discussed and finalized, e.g. *What do you think about our idea for a very strict escape clause for use if sales targets are not reached in the first six months?*
3 Drawing up an outline agreement, e.g. *We will have to insist on a strict escape clause.*

See page ix for the language of meetings.

## The agenda
Students may follow this agenda or change it according to their own judgement.

## Likely outcome

### a) The structure
**Chun**
He clearly has an interest in harnessing the energies of the sales teams that have made him a success in the U.K. However, the X-1 is a very different product and not all typewriter sales people will be able to transfer to computers. It is probably therefore in his interest to devise a selection process to pick out those likely to succeed while not demotivating those who will not. *Option 3* offers dealers a choice of competing for the new dealerships with outsiders. It therefore becomes their choice and he can select under the rules of objective competition. *Option 2* would be second best because the same result would emerge through direct competition for the business sector in the marketplace. But Chun would probably want to keep the High Street store option for the homes sector.

**The dealers**
Many will want the automatic right to market the X-1 in *Option 1* but will realize they are not technically qualified. Others will recognize that they must adapt and learn quickly if they are to succeed. They may therefore prefer *Option 2*. Only the strongest who think they can adapt quickly will accept *Option 3*. Their argument will be that they can apply proven sales records to a new product if Chun helps to finance the training phase.

The most likely outcome will be *Option 3*.

## b) The outline agreement

This will probably include:

i) period of contract, e.g. one year with a six monthly review and six months' notice of termination.

ii) sales targets, e.g. 50 business units per annum.

iii) escape clauses, e.g. termination if sales targets are not reached.

iv) exclusivity clauses, e.g. regional exclusivity or sector exclusivity.

v) discount structure, e.g. 40% discount over 80 business units sold per year.

vi) training, e.g. two weeks' initial training for all staff, two months for technical staff.